POSSESSING THE LAND

by Cherie Noel

PositiveAction
BIBLE CURRICULUM

Possessing the Land – Student Manual

First Edition by Cherie Noel

Copyright © 1990, 2006, 2010, 2020 by Positive Action for Christ, Inc.
P.O. Box 700, 502 W. Pippen Street, Whitakers, NC 27891

positiveaction.org

Fourth Edition, 2020
First Printing
Printed in the United States of America
ISBN: 978-1-59557-337-7

Fourth Edition Writing and Revision
Christa Lord

Editing and Development
Jim Lord

Illustration
Del Thompson

Consulting and Contributions
Helen Boen, C.J. Harris, Nathan Hess, Kristi Houser, Duncan Johnson, Stephanie Smith, Reta Tomkowiak

Additional Graphics and Design
Shannon Brown, Christa Lord, Jim Lord, Jennie Miller, Jesse Snow

Map imagery derived from maps copyright © 2019, Map Resources.

Published by

Contents

Timeline of the Old Testament

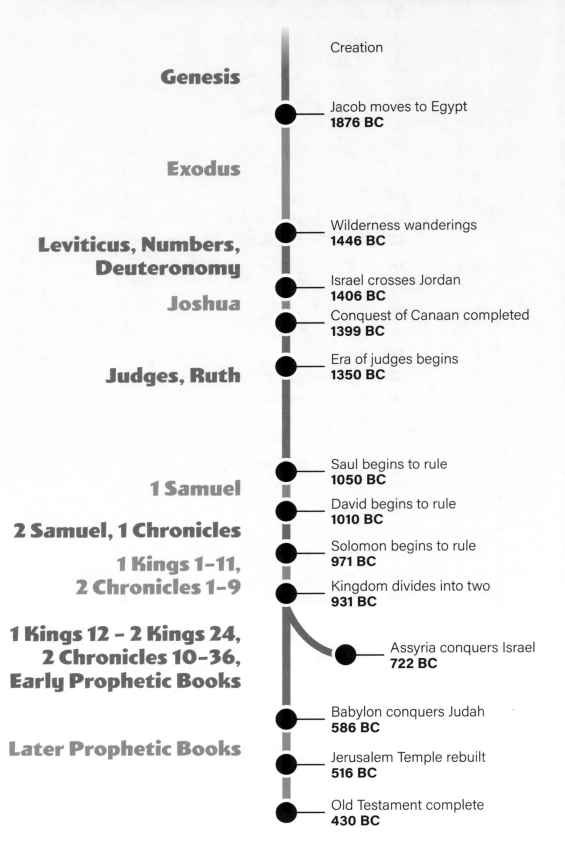

Creation

Genesis

Jacob moves to Egypt
1876 BC

Exodus

Wilderness wanderings
1446 BC

Leviticus, Numbers, Deuteronomy

Israel crosses Jordan
1406 BC

Joshua

Conquest of Canaan completed
1399 BC

Era of judges begins
1350 BC

Judges, Ruth

Saul begins to rule
1050 BC

1 Samuel

David begins to rule
1010 BC

2 Samuel, 1 Chronicles

Solomon begins to rule
971 BC

1 Kings 1–11, 2 Chronicles 1–9

Kingdom divides into two
931 BC

1 Kings 12 – 2 Kings 24, 2 Chronicles 10–36, Early Prophetic Books

Assyria conquers Israel
722 BC

Babylon conquers Judah
586 BC

Later Prophetic Books

Jerusalem Temple rebuilt
516 BC

Old Testament complete
430 BC

LESSON 1
The Word of God

Vocabulary

- **The Bible** – The collection of 66 books inspired by God

- **Scripture** – Sacred writings; another name for the Bible

- **Prophet** – Someone who shares a spiritual message, often from God

- **Prophecy** – A truth said by a prophet; often about future events

- **Inspiration** – The way God worked through human writers to record Scripture; "God-breathed"

- **Testament** – A promise or set of promises; an agreement or covenant

1-A God's Miracle Book

Pick a book off your bookshelf, flip to the title page, and you probably won't see more than one or two authors. Most books are written within a few years by only a few authors.

But when you open your **Bible**, you're looking into a library of **Scripture**—a wealth of books, passages, and poems written by many different authors over 1,600 years. The people who wrote these words were shepherds, rulers, poets, priests, teachers, fishers, and soldiers. Some were educated, and some were not.

Despite so many authors, the Bible is unified. The books fit together well, and we find that a few important ideas come up again and again. In book after book, the Bible tells the same story—God is amazing, and He wants to build a relationship with us.

▶ So how did such a great library fall into our hands? Read **2 Peter 1:20–21**.

⊙ In verse 20, Peter writes that no one made up the prophecies in Scripture.

⊙ Instead, according to verse 21, how did the writers of Scripture speak?

_____

_____

The Bible seems like one story because it has one Author. Before humans wrote anything, God knew it all from the beginning. His Spirit worked through human writers to leave us these books. We call this idea **inspiration**.

► God's words are as reliable as God Himself. Complete the following table.

Verse	What does the verse say about God's Word?
Isaiah 40:8	_____ _____
Matthew 24:35	_____ _____ _____
1 Peter 1:23	_____ _____
After reading these verses, what do you think they say about Scripture?	
_____ _____ _____	

1-B The Beginning and the End

Few things spoil a book more than skipping to the end before you've read the middle. But with the Bible, it helps to know where the story is going. This library of Scripture spreads out like a vast landscape, and sometimes we need a good map.

All of Scripture follows the same big story—how humans turn from God, but God reaches out to us anyway. At the end of time, God will make all things right. So as you read through the ups and downs of the Old Testament, don't forget that there's a good ending.

▶ Look near the beginning of your Bible for the table of contents, which lists all 66 books.

What is the name of the first book?	What is the name of the last book?
_____	_____
A book of beginnings	A book about how God will reveal Himself at the end of time

Look up these verses in the first book and complete the sentences.		Look up these verses in the last book and complete the sentences.	
In the beginning . . .		In the end . . .	
1:1	God creates the heavens and the _____.	**21:1**	The writer John sees a new heaven and _____.
1:5	God calls the light "_____," and He calls the darkness "_____."	**21:25**	The new city of God has no more _____.
1:16	God makes the sun and the moon so we would have light. He also makes the other _____.	**21:23**	The new city does not need the _____ because God Himself shines there.
3:1	The tricky _____ lies to Eve. We learn later that this was Satan, the devil.	**20:10**	The devil who deceived people is thrown into a lake of _____. God defeats him forever.
3:19	Because Adam and Eve sinned, people now suffer and die. We all return to _____.	**21:4**	There is no more _____ _____ _____.
3:23	God sends the first people away from Him, out from the Garden of Eden.	**22:4**	The people in heaven finally get to see _____.

1-C Exploring the Word

The Teacher of Our Hearts

The Bible is sometimes confusing. The books are long, and they use a lot of words we have to look up. But with patience, hard work, and some help from others, we can learn so much from Scripture.

► Thankfully, Christians have plenty of help. We have teachers, family, and leaders from our church, but there's also someone else. Read **John 14:25–26**.

    ◉ Jesus explains that when He is gone, the Father will send the _____, who is the Holy Spirit. (v. 26)

    ◉ The Spirit will teach Jesus' followers _____ and help them remember what Jesus said to them. (v. 26)

► Read **1 Corinthians 2:9–13**, which explains more about the Holy Spirit.

    ◉ Paul explains that the Spirit helped him understand things about God that no one could ever imagine. God's Spirit sees everything, even the _____ of God. (v. 10)

    ◉ Can anyone understand spiritual things without first receiving the Spirit? ☐ Yes ☐ No

► Read **1 Corinthians 3:16** and **Romans 8:9**. If we trust in Christ and receive the Spirit, where does the Spirit live? _____

The Value of Scripture

► What kinds of things do Christians learn from the Spirit? Look up the following passages and complete the table.

Psalm 119:11	We can remember God's Word so we do not _____ against God.
Proverbs 1:1–3	What are some of the things we can learn from the Book of Proverbs? _____ _____
John 20:30–31	Why did John record Jesus' teachings and miracles? So readers would believe that Jesus is the _____, the Son of God—and therefore have life through Him.

▶ In **2 Timothy 3:15–17**, the writer Paul explains the value of Scripture. Using these verses, list at least four of the ways that the Bible can help us grow.

_____

_____

_____

_____

_____

Possessing the Land

▶ Think of one or two big questions you have about the Bible. Write them below, and make time in the next few weeks to research them or ask your teacher.

_____

_____

_____

_____

_____

_____

▶ Ask your teacher or another Christian adult about any advice for studying the Bible. Write your notes below.

_____

_____

_____

_____

_____

_____

_____

LESSON 2
Sin and Redemption

Vocabulary

- **Creation** – Everything God brought into being; the universe

- **Sin** – The decision to break God's law; turning away from God

- **The Fall** – Humanity's turn from God toward sin and death; the results of the first sin

- **Redeem** – To buy back what was lost

2-A Creation and the Fall

Scripture tells the story of its Author, God Himself. The Bible explains how God revealed Himself to the world—most importantly, through the person of Jesus Christ. Everything in Scripture points us to Jesus in some way.

► Read **Genesis 1:26–31** and complete the following.

⊙ After God finishes creating the rest of the world and all the animals, who does God make? (v. 26) _____

⊙ God makes Adam and Eve in His own image, as _____ and _____. (v. 27)

⊙ What does God bless them to do? (v. 28) _____

_____

⊙ God gives them all of **creation** to enjoy, and He knows that everything He made is very _____. (v. 31) Adam, Eve, and God live in peace and happiness together for a time, but this does not last.

► Read **Genesis 2:16–17**. What does God say would happen if Adam ate fruit from the tree of the knowledge of good and evil? _____

▶ Before long, Satan appears as a serpent and tempts Eve to eat the fruit. Read **Genesis 3:1–8** and complete the following table.

Verse 1	The tricky serpent asks the woman if ___god___ really said she should not eat from every tree in the garden.
Verses 2–3	Eve says that she can eat from every tree except the one in the middle of the garden. She says that if she eats the fruit or even touches it, she will ___die___.
Verses 4–5	The serpent tells her that she will not ___certainly want die___ He says that God doesn't want Adam and Eve to understand good and evil.
Verse 6	So Eve looks at the fruit and chooses to eat it. She then gives some of the fruit to ___Adam___, and he eats it, as well.
Verses 7–8	Adam and Eve are ashamed, and they cover themselves with clothing made of ___fig leaves___ They hide when the Lord God comes to talk with them.

Adam and Eve chose to break God's rule. Instead of trusting God's word, they listened to Satan's lies. Instead of enjoying God's gifts, they wanted the one thing they shouldn't have. Because of this decision, they would face the terrible consequences of **sin**. We call this moment **the Fall**, when people first turned away from God.

2-B The Results of Sin

Adam and Eve did not just hurt themselves. Every person throughout history has suffered because of sin—from Adam and Eve's first children all the way down to us today. In Genesis 3 and 4, we read about some of these awful results.

▶ Read **Genesis 3:6–13** and mark the correct ending to the following sentences.

When God walks through the garden, Adam and Eve . . .		
☐ rush to meet Him, happy that He has come to speak with them.	☐ hide behind some trees, out of guilt and fear.	☐ prove to Him that they are just as smart and powerful as He is.

When God asks Adam if he ate fruit from the forbidden tree, Adam . . .		
☐ explains that the fruit helped him become a better husband.	☐ says that he's sorry for disobeying God's command.	☐ blames the woman God gave him.

When God asks Eve to explain what she did, Eve . . .		
☐ blames the serpent for lying to her.	☐ says that she's happier now that she understands ideas like good and evil.	☐ says that she's sorry for ignoring God's warning about the fruit.

▶ Look ahead to **Genesis 3:16–24**. Here God explains to Adam and Eve the results of their sin. In the table below, match the verses to the results they describe.

Verse 16	Verses 17–18	Verse 19	Verses 23–24

Verses	Results of Sin
	People could no longer live in the Garden of Eden.
	Adam would need to work very hard to grow plants or crops.
	Eve would bear children only through pain and suffering. Men and women would try to control each other.
	People would die and return to dust one day.

► Because of their sin, Adam and Eve felt things they never had before. Based on what you've read, how do you think they felt as they talked with God?

⊙ Feelings toward God: _____

⊙ Feelings toward each other: _____

► Read the story of Cain and Abel in **Genesis 4:1–12**.

⊙ Cain doesn't make the right kind of offering to God, and God refuses it. How does Cain feel about that? (v. 5) _____

_____

_____

⊙ So God tells Cain to control himself and guard against sin (vv. 6–7). But what does Cain do instead? (v. 8) _____

_____

_____

_____

► But this doesn't end Adam and Eve's story. According to **Genesis 4:25**, Adam and Eve have another son named _____. His children would learn to pray to God.

2-C The Hope of Redemption

Even though God cast Adam and Eve out of the Garden, He had a plan to bring people back to Himself. Humanity was trapped in sin, and no one could do enough good things to earn a way back into the Garden. So God planned to **redeem** His children. He would pay the price of their sin so they could know Him and walk with Him again.

► Turn back to **Genesis 3:15**. Here God curses the serpent that lied to Eve.

⊙ The snake and the woman would be enemies. Their _____ would also be enemies. Someone would injure the serpent's head, and the serpent would only bruise Him on His _____.

At first, Genesis 3:15 sounds like a promise that a lot of people won't like snakes. But this is not about snakes and people—this is a prophecy about Satan and Jesus.

One day, Jesus Christ would be born to a human mother and grow up to destroy Satan's power. Satan might be allowed to hurt Him a bit, but the serpent would not win.

People from Genesis 1–10

► Look up each verse below and write the name of the person described.

Across

1. Genesis 3:1
The creature who lied to the first woman

5. Genesis 2:7, 20
The first man, made by God from dust

6. Genesis 4:25–26
Adam and Eve's third son, whose children followed God

8. Genesis 10:8–9
A mighty hunter who built many cities after the Great Flood

10. Genesis 5:27
A man who lived 969 years—longer than anyone else in history

Down

2. Genesis 3:20
The first woman and therefore the mother of everyone born since

3. Genesis 6:13
The man God told to build an ark and help save people and animals from the Great Flood

4. Genesis 4:1, 8
The first son and the first murderer

7. Genesis 5:24
A man that walked with God before being taken away

9. Genesis 4:2
A shepherd and the second son of Adam and Eve

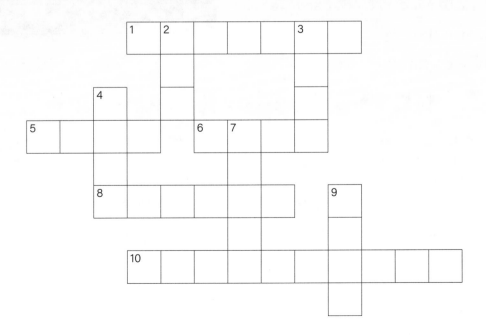

Possessing the Land

If you have trusted Jesus to forgive you for your sins, you don't need to be controlled by anger, guilt, or fear. God has redeemed you back to Himself. If you do something bad, you can run to God, ask His forgiveness, and live like His child again.

▶ Is there ever a good reason to blame others for something we've done wrong? ☐ Yes ☐ No

▶ Is there ever a good reason to hurt others with our anger? ☐ Yes ☐ No

▶ What should you do when someone tells you that you've done something bad?

⊙ If I believe that I've done wrong, I should _____

_____

_____

_____

_____

_____

⊙ If I don't believe I've done something wrong, I should _____

_____

_____

_____

_____

_____

_____

Abraham, Sarah, and Isaac

Vocabulary

- **Hebrews** – God's chosen people; later known as Israelites or Jews

- **Faith** – A belief in something we cannot see or prove; trust in God

- **Covenant** – A binding agreement between two or more people; a promise

- **Famine** – A time when many people have very little food

- **Sacrifice** – To give up something, often to serve or worship God

- **Altar** – A place to offer sacrifices; often a stone mound or table

Humanity fell into sin, but God had a plan to redeem people back to Himself. He chose to send Jesus into the world through one special nation. These chosen people were called **Hebrews**. Later on, they were known as *Israelites* or *Jews*.

Early in the Book of Genesis, this nation did not exist yet. God would build them up through just a few people who were willing to trust Him.

3-A The Call of Abraham

► God chose a man named Abraham to be the father of this new nation. Read **Genesis 12:1–7** and fill in the blanks below.

⊙ Abraham was a wealthy man. He was 75 years old and had many servants and animals. What does God tell him to do? (v. 1) _____

_____

⊙ Does God tell Abraham right away where he needed to go?   ☐ Yes   ☐ No

To follow God, Abraham needed to have **faith**. He needed to trust God for something he couldn't see or feel yet. He had to jump before he knew where he would land.

► God offered Abraham a **covenant**—that is, a promise or agreement. God told Abraham that he and his children would be blessed in great ways. Complete the parts of the covenant below.

Verse	The Promise
Genesis 12:1	God will show Abraham a _____.
Genesis 12:2	God will make from Abraham a great _____.
Genesis 12:3	God will bless those who _____ Abraham, and also curse those who _____ Abraham.
Genesis 12:3	Because of Abraham and his descendants, all the peoples of Earth will be _____.
And later . . .	
Genesis 15:4–5	Through Abraham's own son, God will give him many descendants—just like the _____ in the sky.
Genesis 15:18	God will give Abraham's descendants a land between Egypt's river and the great river called _____.

► Look at **Genesis 15:6**. Why did the Lord call Abraham righteous? _____

_____

3-B Journeys of Abraham and Sarah

► On the next page is a map of the Middle East. This shows some of the places that Abraham and Sarah went during their lifetime. Complete the map by following these instructions:

1. On the western side of the map is the largest body of water, **colored blue**. Label this the **Mediterranean Sea**.

2. There is a **large river** flowing into the Mediterranean Sea from the south, in the country of Egypt. Label this the **Nile River**.

3. The **black dots** mark the location of cities. Look for the city that is farthest north and label it **Haran**.

4. Near Haran are the two rivers called the Tigris and the Euphrates. Follow them both southeast until they meet and flow into each other. Draw a dot near this area to mark a city and label it **Ur**.

5. The **green triangle** near the Mediterranean Sea is a mountain. Label it **Mt. Moriah**.

6. There is one city a little north of Mt. Moriah. Label it **Bethel**.

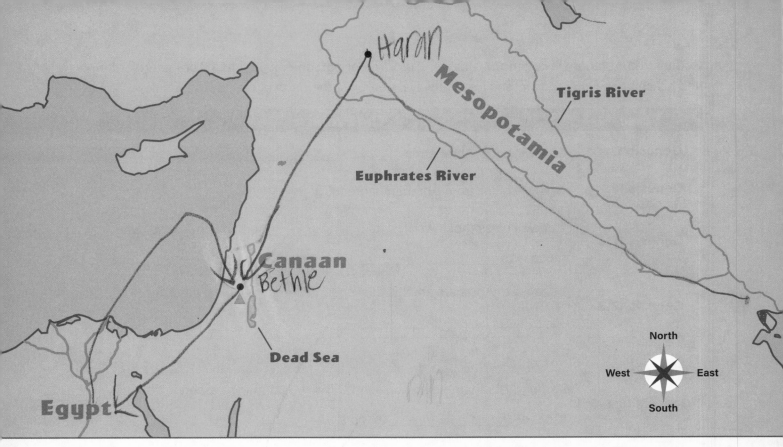

► Read the verses below and fill in the blanks. Then draw four lines on the map to show the routes taken by Abraham and Sarah.

Verse	Route
Genesis 11:31	Abraham's father took the family from **Ur** to **H**aran.
Genesis 12:7–8	After hearing God's call, Abraham and Sarah journeyed southwest toward Canaan. God said that He would give this land to Abraham's descendants. So Abraham camped east of the city of **B**ethle.
Genesis 12:10	During a *famine*, Abraham decided to stay in **E**gypt.
Genesis 13:1–3	Later, Abraham and Sarah left Egypt to travel through the Negev region. Once again, they set their tents near **B**ethle.

► After a while, Abraham and his nephew Lot separated their flocks and went different directions. Abraham chose to remain in Canaan, and God appeared to him again. Read **Genesis 13:14–17** and summarize God's promise to Abraham.

_____

_____

_____

3-C God Provides for Isaac

Abraham and Sarah waited a long time before God fulfilled His promise of a son. When Sarah was about 90 years old, she gave birth to a baby boy. Abraham named him *Isaac*, which means "laughter."

► Even though God had finally given Abraham and Sarah a son, He had not finished testing their faith. Read **Genesis 22:1-19** and use the words below to complete the story.

Abraham	altar	angel	Isaac	knife	lamb	Moriah	ram	wood

God chose to test _____Abraham_____'s trust in Him. God told Abraham to take his son _____Isaac_____ to the land of _____Moriah_____ and offer him as a sacrifice on one of the mountains there. Killing your children is wrong, so Abraham may have been confused. But he chose to obey anyway.

Abraham and Isaac traveled for three days before reaching the mountain. They started to walk up, leaving behind their donkey with the servants. Isaac carried _____wood_____, while Abraham held the fire and the _____knife_____. Isaac asked his father where they would find a _____lamb_____ to offer. Abraham replied that God would provide one.

When they reached the place, Abraham bound Isaac and laid him on the _____altar_____ and the wood. Even though Isaac was his very own son, Abraham picked up the knife to kill him. But an _____angel_____ of the Lord called out to Abraham and stopped him. Abraham had proven that he feared God and would give up anything for Him.

Abraham looked up and saw a _____ram_____ caught in a nearby thicket. God had provided His own sacrifice to take Isaac's place.

▶ Many years later, Abraham sent a servant back to his homeland to find a wife for Isaac. The servant promised to do everything he could to bring a woman back, so long as she was willing. Read **Genesis 24:10-22** and answer the questions.

⊙ The servant wanted God to show him which woman would be a good wife for Isaac. What did the servant hope this woman would do? (vv. 13–14)

_____

_____

⊙ Who showed kindness to the servant? (v. 15) _____

⊙ What did the servant give her as thanks? (v. 22) _____

_____

⊙ Look ahead to **verse 58**. Did Rebekah decide to go and marry Isaac? ☐ Yes ☐ No

⊙ Read **verses 62–67**. Was Isaac happy to meet Rebekah? ☐ Yes ☐ No

Possessing the Land

Abraham, Sarah, Isaac, Rebekah, and the servant all showed great faith to do what God wanted them to do. Like everyone else, they sinned and made mistakes, but they trusted God to fulfill what He promised.

▶ Write one way your faith is being tested right now. How can you show that you trust God?

_____

_____

_____

_____

_____

LESSON 4
Jacob and Esau

Vocabulary

- **Firstborn** – The first child of a husband and wife

- **Birthright** – The benefits and privileges of the eldest child, usually the firstborn son; often a greater inheritance or place of leadership

- **Blessing** – Giving someone special favor or grace; words that wish happiness or success

- **Israel** – The name given to Jacob and his descendants; means "wrestling with God"

4-A Selling the Birthright

Isaac and Rebekah had twin sons—Jacob and Esau. The two brothers grew up to be very different. Esau loved to hunt in the fields, but Jacob enjoyed staying close to home. Isaac liked Esau the best, while Rebekah favored Jacob.

Esau was considered the eldest, or **firstborn**, because he was born a few moments before Jacob. In ancient times, parents treated the firstborn differently than the other siblings. For example, the firstborn had a special **birthright**, meaning that he would inherit much more property than his brothers and sisters.

▶ Read the story in **Genesis 25:27–34** and answer the questions.

⊙ What is Jacob doing when Esau comes back from the fields?

_____

⊙ What does Esau want? _____

⊙ How does Jacob get Esau to give up the birthright? _____

_____

_____

▶ Think about what Jacob and Esau do in this story. What can you tell about their attitudes?

What does Jacob think of Esau?	Does Esau value his birthright? How do you know?
_____	_____
_____	_____
_____	_____
_____	_____
_____	_____
_____	_____

4-B Stealing the Blessing

Remember that God gave Abraham and Isaac many promises and blessings. Isaac planned to pass on these blessings to his favorite son, Esau. Even though Jacob now had the birthright, Esau would at least carry on the family's spiritual legacy.

But Rebekah remembered a promise God gave her long ago—that her older son would serve the younger. She wanted to make this promise happen herself. So she decided to help trick Isaac into giving Jacob the blessing.

▶ Read **Genesis 27:1–29** and match each sentence to its correct ending.

Verse 1—Isaac was old, and he could no longer . . .	**A.** place animal skins on Jacob's hands and neck.
Verses 3–4—Isaac asked Esau to . . .	**B.** hunt and prepare some food.
Verses 9–10—Rebekah then told Jacob to . . .	**C.** lie and say he was.
Verses 16, 23—To trick Isaac, Rebekah chose to . . .	**D.** see.
Verse 24—When Isaac asked if he was Esau, Jacob followed the plan to . . .	**E.** rule over his brothers.
Verse 29—Isaac said that Jacob would . . .	**F.** bring food to Isaac and get the blessing instead of Esau.

▶ Read **verses 34 and 38**. How does Esau feel when he hears that Jacob had stolen the blessing?

_____

_____

▶ In **verses 41–45**, what does Rebekah tell Jacob to do? Why?

_____

_____

_____

So Jacob left his home, traveling toward Haran to stay with his uncle Laban. This man was Rebekah's brother—the one who talked with Abraham's servant. Jacob hoped to find a wife in Haran like his father had. Isaac had told Jacob not to marry anyone from the wicked families in Canaan.

One night on the way to Haran, Jacob dreamed of a strange ladder or stairway reaching up into heaven, with angels going up and down to the ground. Standing above it all was God, who made some promises to Jacob.

▶ Read **Genesis 28:10-17**. Below are the promises that God offered to Abraham, Jacob's grandfather. Which of these promises did God pass on to Jacob?

Promised to Abraham	Promised to Jacob?	
God will make him a great nation, with many descendants.	☐ Yes	☐ No
God will give his descendants a land.	☐ Yes	☐ No
Through his descendants, all the peoples of the world will be blessed.	☐ Yes	☐ No

▶ Based on what you've read, do you think that Jacob deserved these promises? ☐ Yes ☐ No

▶ If not, why do you think God offered this covenant to Jacob?

_____

_____

_____

_____

4-C Wrestling with God

▶ Jacob reached Haran and was happy to find Laban and his family. Unfortunately, Laban was as tricky and dishonest as Jacob had been. Read **Genesis 29:14–30** and mark the correct ending to each sentence below.

Laban offers to pay Jacob, but Jacob instead wants to work . . .

☐ for free.	☐ seven years to marry Rachel.	☐ seven years to marry Leah.

Jacob works for Laban, and the years feel like . . .

☐ decades because he hates the work.	☐ weeks because he is a fast worker.	☐ days because he loves Rachel.

At the end of Jacob's work, Laban throws a feast and . . .

☐ gives Rachel to be Jacob's wife.	☐ gives Zilpah to be Jacob's wife.	☐ gives Leah to be Jacob's wife.

After Laban makes excuses for his trickery, Jacob . . .

☐ marries Rachel too, and then works another seven years.	☐ chooses to love his new wife, Leah.	☐ brings Laban before a judge.

Now married to more than one wife, Jacob . . .

☐ knows that he has done something wrong.	☐ loves both wives equally.	☐ loves Rachel more than Leah.

Many years later, Jacob decided to leave Haran. Because Jacob had made Laban rich, Laban made it very difficult for Jacob to leave. But Jacob finally took his family and wealth from his father-in-law and traveled back to Canaan. With him were all his wives, children, servants, and animals.

▶ On the way, Jacob heard that Esau was coming to meet him with an army of four hundred men. Read Jacob's prayer in **Genesis 32:9–12**.

⊙ How does Jacob describe himself to God? (v. 10) _____

_____

⊙ So why does Jacob expect God to protect him? (vv. 11–12) _____

_____

_____

► That night, when Jacob thought he was alone, a mysterious man appeared and wrestled with him. Read **Genesis 32:24–31**.

⊙ What name does this person give Jacob? (v. 28) _____

⊙ Who does Jacob believe this person to be? (v. 30) _____

God kept His promises to Jacob. Esau did not attack Jacob but instead offered his brother kindness and friendship. They wept together after being apart for so long.

Possessing the Land

► There's an important principle in **Galatians 6:7**. Write this verse below:

_____

_____

_____

_____

In this verse, the Apostle Paul means that we will face the consequences of our actions. If we plant the seeds of sin, the fruits of sin will grow. Sin will always hurt us and the people around us. Some call this the Principle of Sowing and Reaping.

► Choose one of the following people and explain a time when they reaped what they had sown.

Rebekah	Esau	Jacob	Laban

_____

_____

_____

_____

_____

_____

► How would patience have helped this person?

_____

_____

_____

_____

LESSON 5
The Trials of Joseph

Vocabulary

- **Polygamy** – Having more than one wife

- **Sheaf / Sheaves** – Bundles of grain gathered and tied together during harvest

- **Slave** – Someone who works for no pay, often a captive against their will

- **Pharaoh** – A king or queen of Egypt; often claimed to be a god

5-A Joseph the Little Brother

Jacob was greatly blessed by God, but he also had many problems in his family. Besides the children he had through his wives, Leah and Rachel, he also had children through two of their servants, Bilhah and Zilpah. Many people in these days practiced **polygamy**, but this was a very bad decision that created a lot of jealousy and conflict.

▶ Read **Genesis 35:23–26** and list the twelve sons of Jacob under their mothers.

Leah	Bilhah	Rachel
1.	1.	1.
2.	2.	2.
3.		
4.	Zilpah	
5.	1.	
6.	2.	

► Joseph was the youngest of all his brothers, except for Benjamin. Read **Genesis 37:1-11** and fill in the blanks to explain why Joseph was hated by his older brothers.

Verse 2	After helping his brothers care for the flock, Joseph brings to his father _____.
Verses 3–4	Jacob _____ Joseph more than the others, and he gives Joseph a special set of clothes.
Verses 5–8	Joseph tells his brothers about a _____ in which their **sheaves** of grain bowed down to his own.
Verses 9–11	Joseph dreams another where the _____, _____, and eleven stars bowed to him. This time, even Jacob rebukes him.

► The brothers' hatred for Joseph continued to boil until one day, they decided to act on it. Read the story in **Genesis 37:12–36**, and then number the events from 1 to 10 in the order they happened. The first is already marked.

	Reuben returns to the pit to rescue Joseph, but finds him gone.
	Joseph doesn't find his brothers in Shechem, but hears that they went to Dothan.
	Judah convinces his brothers to sell Joseph as a **slave**.
1	Jacob tells Joseph to check on his brothers as they watch the flock in Shechem.
	The brothers take Joseph's clothes and throw him into a pit.
	The brothers tell Jacob that Joseph must have been killed, and Jacob mourns.
	The brothers eat some food, and they notice some traders heading toward Egypt.
	Reuben convinces his brothers to throw Joseph into a pit or well, instead of killing him.
	The brothers decide to cover up their sin by dipping Joseph's coat in goat blood.
	The brothers see Joseph coming, and they plan how they can kill him.

5-B Joseph the Slave

The traders took Joseph southwest to Egypt, where they sold him as if he were an animal or piece of property. Joseph was bought by Potiphar, an important man who served as the captain of **Pharaoh's** guards.

As a captive and a slave, Joseph had to do whatever he was told. He did not own anything, even his own clothing. No matter how hard he worked, he would probably never be able to free himself and go back home. He was trapped in a land filled with wicked people who did not care about him or his God.

► Take a moment to imagine yourself in Joseph's place.

⊙ How hard would you work for Potiphar? _____

⊙ How often would you think about what your brothers did? _____

⊙ Would it be easy to forget about God? _____

► Read **Genesis 39:1–21** and use the words below to complete the story. Some words will appear more than once.

wife	Lord	garment	Potiphar	sin

The _____ was with Joseph, so he prospered and succeeded in whatever he did. Eventually, _____ put Joseph in charge of the entire household. Joseph's master didn't have to worry about anything.

Unfortunately, Joseph also got the attention of Potiphar's _____. She thought Joseph was handsome and tried to commit adultery with him. He told her that he could never do such a thing because it would be very wicked and a _____ against God. When she caught him alone one day, he ran away from her, leaving part of his _____ in her hand.

Angry at being told no, Potiphar's _____ screamed and said that Joseph had attacked her. She used his _____ as evidence for her lie.

When _____ heard this, he threw Joseph into prison. But even there, the _____ was with Joseph.

5-C Joseph the Prisoner

Maybe the only thing worse than being a slave was being a prisoner. Joseph had done nothing wrong, but he found himself in Pharaoh's private dungeon anyway. But during this dark time, God shone through Joseph all the brighter.

► Compare **Genesis 39:2–6** and **39:20–23**. Even though Joseph was thrown out of Potiphar's house into prison, name at least two things that do *not* change.

⊙ _____

_____

⊙ _____

_____

► Read **Genesis 40:1–8**. When Pharaoh throws his cupbearer and baker into prison, how does Joseph show them kindness? (vv. 4, 7–8)

_____

_____

► God shows Joseph the meaning for each of the two dreams. Use the verses in **Genesis 40** to fill in the blanks below.

The Cupbearer	
Verses 9–11 – The Dream	**Verses 12–13** – The Meaning
He sees a vine with _____ branches. He picks some _____, presses them into a cup, and gives the cup to _____.	In _____ days, he will again serve _____ as cupbearer.

The Baker	
Verses 16–17 – The Dream	**Verses 18–19** – The Meaning
He has _____ baskets that he carries on his _____. But some _____ eat all the baked goods inside.	In _____ days, he will be executed by _____ and be eaten by _____.

► What does Joseph ask the cupbearer to do for him? (v. 14) _____

_____

► Does the cupbearer remember to do this? (v. 23) ☐ Yes ☐ No

Possessing the Land

► Can you think of a time when you did something good, but bad things happened anyway? What happened when you tried to do right, but everything went wrong?

_____

_____

_____

_____

_____

► If bad things can still happen even when we try to do good, why should we still do good?

_____

_____

_____

_____

LESSON 6
The Mercy of Joseph

Vocabulary

- **_Tribe_** – A group of people united together; usually related through a shared ancestor

6-A Joseph Finds Peace

After the cupbearer was freed from prison, Joseph spent two more years waiting for help. Then one night, Pharaoh had two strange dreams.

▶ Words can barely describe how strange these dreams were. Read **Genesis 41:1–7**, pick one dream, and try to draw a picture of it below:

After hearing about the dream, the cupbearer remembered Joseph and told Pharaoh about him. So Pharaoh's servants quickly took Joseph out of prison, cleaned him up, gave him new clothes, and brought him to Pharaoh.

▶ When Pharaoh asks Joseph if he can interpret dreams, what does Joseph say? Summarize **Genesis 41:16** in your own words.

_____

_____

_____

▶ What did the dreams mean? Use **Genesis 41:25–32** to describe the meaning of each part.

	Parts of the Dream	Meaning
Verses 26, 29	Seven good cows and good ears of corn	
Verse 27	Seven thin cows and unhealthy ears of corn	
Verses 29–31	The unhealthy eating up the healthy	

Joseph advised Pharaoh to appoint someone to gather food for seven years so that when the famine came, Egypt would be ready. Pharaoh and his advisors thought that this was a good idea.

▶ Look at **Genesis 41:38–40**. Why does Pharaoh choose Joseph to prepare Egypt for the famine?

_____

_____

▶ After all the trouble Joseph endured, it seems he found some peace. He also married Asenath, the daughter of a priest, and they had two sons. According to **Genesis 41:50–52**, what did the name of each son mean?

⊙ **Manasseh:** _____

_____

_____

⊙ **Ephraim:** _____

_____

_____

6-B Joseph Forgives His Brothers

After seven years, when the famine finally came, it hurt not only Egypt but also Canaan. Joseph's brothers and their families needed food. So when Jacob heard that the Egyptians had grain, he sent all of Joseph's brothers to Egypt—all except Benjamin, that is.

▶ Read the passages below and fill in the blanks.

Genesis 42:6–8	When Joseph's brothers come to Egypt, they _____ down to him, but they do not _____ him.
Genesis 42:9–15	Joseph decides to test his brothers, so he accuses them of being _____. He tells them to prove him wrong by bringing their _____ to Egypt.
	Joseph allows the brothers to buy food for their families, but he holds Simeon in Egypt to make sure they return with Benjamin.
Genesis 42:35–36	After they get home, the brothers find their _____ still in their packs. If they go back to Egypt, they might be arrested as thieves. _____ believes that he'll never see Simeon again.
	The famine gets much worse, so Jacob allows the brothers to take Benjamin to Egypt and buy more food.
Genesis 43:29–31	When Joseph sees Benjamin after all this time, he has to go to another room to _____.
Genesis 44:1–5	Joseph sends the brothers away again with their food and their money. But this time, he tells his steward to place a _____ in Benjamin's pack.
Genesis 44:18–34	The Egyptians accuse the brothers of stealing and bring them back to Egypt. When Joseph threatens to keep Benjamin as a slave, _____ offers to stay in his younger brother's place.
Genesis 45:1–5	Joseph can control himself no longer. He says, "I am _____" and asks if his father is still alive. The brothers are _____, but Joseph comforts them.

6-C Joseph Cares for His Family

When Joseph's brothers realized that the boy they sold into slavery was now the ruler of Egypt—second only to Pharaoh himself—they were terrified. Joseph could have done anything he wanted to them.

▶ But in this moment Joseph revealed exactly the kind of person he was. Read **Genesis 45:5–8**. What does Joseph think about all the troubles he endured?

_____

_____

_____

_____

So Joseph took care of his brothers and all their families. He brought everyone to Egypt, and Jacob finally got to see his long lost son. Jacob also met his two new grandsons, Ephraim and Manasseh. Jacob blessed them as if they were equal to his own fully grown sons.

The Egyptians didn't usually like Hebrews, but Pharaoh allowed all of them to stay in the land of Goshen, the part of Egypt closest to Canaan. There the children of Israel grew and multiplied for many years. God used Joseph and Egypt to turn a small family into a gigantic nation.

▶ When Joseph was old and nearing his death, he looked ahead to the day when Israel would leave Egypt and claim the land that God promised them. Read **Genesis 50:22–25**. What does Joseph make his family promise him? (v. 25)

_____

_____

The Twelve Tribes of Israel

▶ Over many years, the sons of Israel became the *tribes* of Israel. Use the clues to fill in their names.

⊙ **Genesis 29:32** – ⬜⬜⬜⬜⬜⬜ was the first son of Jacob and Leah.

⊙ **Genesis 30:5–6** – ⬜⬜⬜ was Bilhah's first son.

⊙ **Genesis 30:7–8** – ⬜⬜⬜⬜⬜⬜⬜ was Bilhah's second son.

⊙ **Genesis 30:11** – ⬜⬜⬜ was the first son of Zilpah.

⊙ **Genesis 35:18** – ⬜⬜⬜⬜⬜⬜⬜⬜ was Rachel's second son.

⊙ **Genesis 41:51** – ⬜⬜⬜⬜⬜⬜⬜ was Joseph's first son.

⊙ **Genesis 42:24** – Joseph held ⬜⬜⬜⬜⬜ for a while in Egypt.

⊙ **Genesis 44:18** – ⬜⬜⬜⬜⬜ offered to take Benjamin's punishment.

⊙ **Genesis 48:14** – Jacob blessed ⬜⬜⬜⬜⬜⬜⬜ over his brother.

⊙ **Genesis 49:13** – Jacob promised ⬜⬜⬜⬜⬜⬜ a land by the sea.

⊙ **Genesis 49:14** – ⬜⬜⬜⬜⬜⬜⬜ showed great strength.

⊙ **Genesis 49:20** – Jacob promised that ⬜⬜⬜⬜ would be wealthy.

▶ Use the letters in the blue boxes above to complete this sentence:

God ⬜⬜⬜⬜⬜⬜ **those who wait on Him.**

Possessing the Land

▶ Joseph's view of his troubles sounds a lot like one verse in the New Testament: **Romans 8:28**. Can this verse make it easier for you to forgive people who do bad things to you? Why or why not?

_____

_____

_____

_____

_____

_____

Israel in Bondage

Vocabulary

- **Taskmaster / Slave master** – A person who oversees slaves; someone who forces others to work

- **Mortar** – A substance to hold bricks together; usually a mixture of sand, water, and other minerals

- **Midwife** – A woman who helps pregnant mothers give birth to their babies

- **Sojourner** – Someone living in a foreign land for a while

- **Yahweh** – The holiest name of God used by ancient Hebrews; means "I AM"

7-A The Hebrews Enslaved

▶ Read **Exodus 1:1–10** and answer the following questions.

⊙ How many people do Joseph and his brothers first bring to Egypt? (v. 5) _____

⊙ What happens to the Israelites over many years? (v. 7)

_____

_____

_____

⊙ What does the new king of Egypt think about the people of Israel? (vv. 8–10)

_____

_____

_____

⊙ According to verse 8, this king does not know about _____.

▶ With a mixture of fear and hatred, the Egyptians started to oppress and enslave the Hebrews. To see what Egypt did to Israel, read **Exodus 1:11–16** and fill in the blanks.

Verse 11	The Egyptians decide to place _____ over the Israelites to force them to build cities for Pharaoh.
Verses 13–14	Bit by bit, the Egyptians make the Israelites' lives terrible, forcing them to work in _____, in brick, and in the fields.
Verses 15–16	The king of Egypt also tells the Hebrew **midwives** to kill any _____ born to the Israelites.

▶ Read **Exodus 1:17–22**. Do you think the midwives did the right thing? Why or why not?

_____

_____

_____

_____

_____

7-B The Birth of Moses

▶ Read the story in **Exodus 2:1–10** and mark the correct endings to the following sentences.

There is a husband and wife who are both descendants of . . .		
☐ Reuben.	☐ Judah.	☐ Levi.

The woman gives birth to a baby boy. When she can't hide him any longer . . .		
☐ she places him in a basket near the banks of the Nile River.	☐ she hands him over to the Egyptians.	☐ she tells everyone that he is a girl.

The baby is found by . . .

- [ ] crocodiles.
- [ ] a group of Egyptian soldiers.
- [ ] Pharaoh's daughter.

They are all being watched by . . .

- [ ] Pharaoh.
- [ ] the baby's sister.
- [ ] a bored cat licking its paws.

Pharaoh's daughter lets the baby be . . .

- [ ] handed over to the Egyptians.
- [ ] nursed by a woman who happened to be the baby's mother.
- [ ] put back into the Nile River.

▶ Pharaoh's daughter eventually adopted the baby and called him Moses. Read **Exodus 2:11–22** and use the words below to complete the story.

afraid	Egyptian	Gershom	Hebrew	judge	Midian	sand	Zipporah

One day, after Moses was grown, he went out to see the work done by his fellow Hebrews. He saw an Egyptian beating a _____. After looking to see if anyone was watching, Moses killed the _____ and hid the body in the _____.

The next day, Moses tried to stop two Hebrews from fighting. They jeered at him and asked who had made him a prince or _____ over them. Was Moses going to kill them like he had killed that Egyptian?

Then Moses was _____. Others must know what he did.

When Pharaoh found out, he tried to kill Moses. But Moses ran away from Egypt to the land of _____, where he met seven sisters and helped them water their father's flock. He married one of them, a woman named _____. They called their son _____, which means "stranger" or "***sojourner***."

7-C The Call of Moses

▶ By the time Moses was a grown man, the people of Israel had spent hundreds of years in Egypt. Look at **Exodus 2:23–25**. After all this time, what did the people do?

_____

_____

▶ Did God hear them? ☐ Yes ☐ No

▶ Read the following passages and mark each sentence as true or false. If the sentence is false, re-write it correctly in the space below.

☐ True ☐ False	**Exodus 3:1–6** – God tells Moses to remove his coat because he is in a holy place.

Correction: _____

_____

☐ True ☐ False	**Exodus 3:7–9** – God asks Moses how the Israelites are doing.

Correction: _____

_____

☐ True ☐ False	**Exodus 3:10** – God tells Moses to go to Pharaoh and lead Israel out of Egypt.

Correction: _____

_____

☐ True ☐ False	**Exodus 3:11–12** – Moses agrees that he's the best person to lead Israel.

Correction: _____

_____

☐ True ☐ False	**Exodus 3:13–14** – God calls Himself "I AM."

Correction: _____

_____

☐ True ☐ False	**Exodus 4:1–9** – God gives Moses a few signs or miracles to show Pharaoh and the people.

Correction: _____

_____

☐ True ☐ False	**Exodus 4:10–17** – When Moses complains that he cannot speak well, God gives up on him and talks to someone else.

Correction: _____

_____

Possessing the Land

► Think about the kind of courage showed by the midwives, by Moses' sister, and eventually by Moses himself. All of these people had to take risks to do what they knew to be right. In the space below, describe something that you know you should do, but you're (at least a little) scared of doing. What has God given you to help conquer that fear?

_____

_____

_____

_____

_____

_____

_____

LESSON 8
The Exodus from Egypt

Vocabulary

- **Idol** – A statue or image of a false god; often worshiped

- **Symbol** – Something that represents or pictures another idea

- **Plague** – A disaster for a large number of people; in Scripture, often reveals God's judgment

- **Boil** – A painful infection in the skin that raises as it fills with dead cells and pus

- **Locust** – A grasshopper that can become agitated and begin to swarm, often damaging crops

- **Passover** – A Jewish holiday celebrating the day God rescued the Israelites from Egypt

- **Unleavened Bread** – Bread that has no yeast or has not been allowed to rise

- **Exodus** – Leaving or departing a place; Israel's departure from Egypt

8-A The Plagues

The Egyptians trusted in false gods. The rulers and priests made up many different gods, built **idols** to represent them, and forced the people to worship them. The people also thought that many things around them were **symbols** of their gods. So they honored the Sun and the Nile River—and even things like cows, frogs, cats, and flies. These religions helped the rulers stay in power. Many Pharaohs even claimed to be gods.

So when Moses told Pharaoh that God said to let Israel go, Pharaoh didn't care. The king asked why he should obey this God he had never known.

▶ Read **Exodus 7:1–5**, paying close attention to verses 4–5. In your own words, why was God going to show Egypt His signs and wonders?

_____

_____

_____

▶ So God sent ten *plagues* or disasters on Egypt. He showed everyone that He had power over all the gods that the Egyptians thought were real. In the following chart, look up each passage, describe the plague, and answer the rest of the questions.

	Description of the Plague	Response to the Plague
Plague 1 **Exodus 7:19–25**	Verses 20–21	Can the magicians copy this sign? ☐ Yes ☐ No Pharaoh's heart _____ _____.
Plague 2 **Exodus 8:1–15**	Verse 6	Can the magicians copy this sign? ☐ Yes ☐ No Pharaoh promises to let Israel go if God gets rid of the _____. Does he keep this promise? ☐ Yes ☐ No
Plague 3 **Exodus 8:16–19**	Verse 17	Can the magicians copy this sign? ☐ Yes ☐ No The magicians tell Pharaoh that this plague is the _____ _____.
Plague 4 **Exodus 8:20–32**	Verse 24	Why does God keep this plague away from His people? _____ _____ _____ _____
Plague 5 **Exodus 9:1–7**	Verse 6	Does this plague hurt Israel? ☐ Yes ☐ No Pharaoh's heart is still _____ _____.

	Description of the Plague	Response to the Plague
Plague 6 **Exodus 9:8–12**	Verse 10	Do the magicians have any power over this plague? ☐ Yes ☐ No How can you tell? _____ _____ _____ _____.
Plague 7 **Exodus 9:22–35**	Verses 23–25	Pharaoh admits that he has _____. (v. 27) Does he let Israel go after the plague ends? ☐ Yes ☐ No
Plague 8 **Exodus 10:12–20**	Verses 14–15	Pharaoh again says that he has _____, and he asks Moses and Aaron to forgive him and end the plague. (v. 16) Does he let Israel go after the plague ends? ☐ Yes ☐ No
Plague 9 **Exodus 10:21–29**	Verses 22–23	Does this plague hurt Israel? ☐ Yes ☐ No What does Pharaoh tell Moses to do? (v. 28) _____ _____ _____ _____

At this point, Egypt had endured nine plagues, and Pharaoh still would not let Israel go. God always knew that Pharaoh would resist Him, so He sent a tenth and final plague to strike Egypt.

8-B The Passover

▶ God told Moses and his brother Aaron to prepare the people for the final plague. Read **Exodus 12:1-11** and fill in the blanks below.

Verses 3-5	Every household needed to find a perfect male _____. If the household was too small, they could share one with others.
Verses 6-7	Later that month, the people should _____ the animal and spread some of the blood around the doors of their houses.
Verse 8	The people should eat the roasted meat with _____ _____.
Verse 11	The people should keep everything they need to travel nearby, and they should eat their food _____.

▶ Look further at **verses 12-13** and then **verses 21-27**. In your own words, why do people remember this day as the **Passover**?

_____

_____

_____

▶ Finish reading the story in **verses 28-42** and fill in the blanks below.

The people of Israel did what the _____ told them to do. At midnight, the
<verse 28>

Lord killed every _____ in Egypt, except for those in a house with
<verse 29>

blood on the door. All the Egyptians cried out in sorrow, and _____
<verses 30-31>

summoned Moses and Aaron. He told them to go with Israel to worship the Lord.

Scared for their lives, the _____ pushed the Israelites to leave
<verse 33>

quickly. The people did not even have time to let their bread rise. God made the Egyptians

give up their riches happily, so the Israelites _____ them.
<verse 36>

When the Israelites left Egypt, they had lived there _____ years. They would
<verse 40>

remember this night as the time that the _____ brought them out of Egypt.
<verse 42>

8-C The Exodus

▶ Follow the instructions below to fill in the map.

- ◉ Label the **Mediterranean Sea**, the **body of water** along the northern edge of the map.

- ◉ Label the **Nile**, the **river** flowing along the western edge of the map into the Mediterranean.

- ◉ Label **Egypt**, the **land** around the Nile River.

- ◉ In the southeast is a large **body of water** that almost looks like a rabbit head with two long ears sticking up. Label the head the **Red Sea**.

- ◉ Label the rabbit's **western ear** the **Gulf of Suez**, and label the **eastern ear** the **Gulf of Aqaba**.

- ◉ Label the **Sinai Peninsula**, the **land** that juts south between the two ears of the Red Sea.

- ◉ The **green triangle** in the Sinai Peninsula is probably the site of **Mount Sinai**. Label this, too.

- ◉ Label **Canaan**, the **land** in the northeast between the Mediterranean and the Dead Sea.

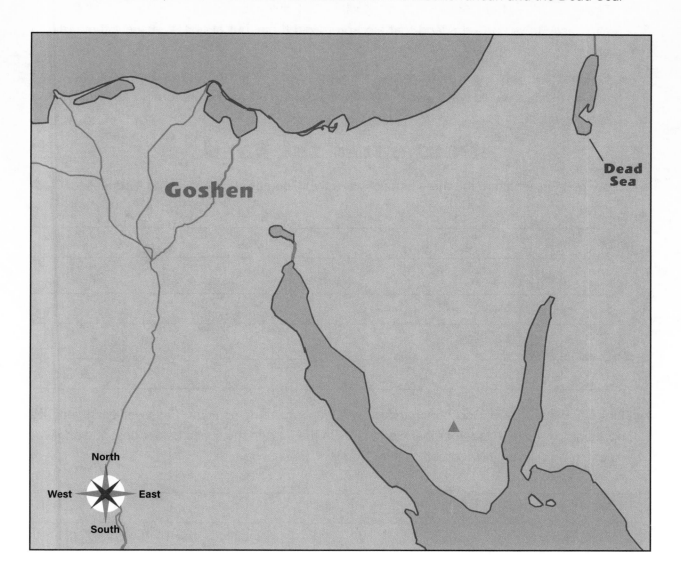

A few days after Israel left Egypt, Pharaoh regretted that he had let them go. So he chased after the people with an army of chariots and horses. The Israelites feared that they were trapped between the Egyptians and the Red Sea, but God sent a strong wind to roll back the water. Israel crossed over on dry land, and when the Egyptians tried to follow, the water flowed back and drowned the entire army. God had saved Israel.

To thank God, Moses and the people of Israel offered a song of praise (Exo. 15:1–18). Moses' sister Miriam, who served as a prophetess, sang and danced with all the women (Exo. 15:20–21).

► Follow the instructions below to draw the route taken by the people of Israel.

   ⊙ After Passover, the Israelites traveled from a placed called Rameses to Succoth (Exo. 12:37). Today, we don't know exactly where these places are, but draw an arrow from **Goshen** to the northern end of the **Gulf of Suez**. This might be where the Israelites crossed the Red Sea.

   ⊙ Now draw an arrow from the **Red Sea crossing** southeast toward **Mount Sinai**. The people of Israel lived near this mountain for about a year, and it was here that God gave them His Law.

   ⊙ Draw an arrow from **Sinai** north along the Gulf of Aqaba toward **Canaan**. The Israelites eventually traveled to the land that God promised them, but at first, they were too afraid to enter.

   ⊙ So from **Canaan**, draw an arrow back toward the northern tip of the **Gulf of Aqaba**. The people of Israel would wander in the wilderness for forty years before turning back toward the promised land.

Possessing the Land

► In your opinion, what are the three biggest ways that God has shown love and kindness to you?

   ⊙ _____
   _____

   ⊙ _____
   _____

   ⊙ _____
   _____

► Think back about how God commanded His people to remember the Passover each year. It's important to take time to remember God's work in the past. In the space below, describe one way you can regularly remind yourself of what God has done for you.

_____

_____

_____

LESSON 9
The Law of God

Vocabulary

- **Law** – A rule that shows how to apply a moral idea or principle; God's instructions to His people

- **Commandment** – Another name for a law; in Exodus, the Ten Commandments begin God's Law

- **Sabbath** – The seventh day of the week; means "rest;" the day God rested after creating the world

- **False Witness / False Testimony** – A deception or lie told to others

- **Covet** – To want something that does not belong to you, even if you should not have it

- **Tabernacle** – In Scripture, a tent compound where God showed His presence to Israel

9-A The Ten Commandments

God's people had lived in Egypt for over 400 years. During this time, they had no word from God. Some of the Israelites still worshiped God, but many had forgotten what He promised to their ancestors. They did not know what He expected from them or what He planned for them. Instead, they followed the rules and customs of the Egyptians.

But God wanted to set His people apart from the sinful, wicked nations around them. He showed them how to live in a more loving and righteous way. He taught them about His righteousness, even if they could not come close to reaching it.

► While the people waited around Mount Sinai, God called Moses up to hear the **Law**. The simplest and most important of these instructions are the **Ten Commandments**. Read them in **Exodus 20:1–17** and complete the following summaries.

The First Verses 2–3	Do not have any other _____ before Me.
The Second Verses 4–6	Do not make any _____ of anything in the sky, earth, or sea. Do not worship them.

The Third Verse 7	Do not _____ the name of God disrespectfully.
The Fourth Verses 8–11	Remember the _____ day, to keep it holy. Rest on this day, just as God did after creating the world.
The Fifth Verse 12	_____ your father and mother.
The Sixth Verse 13	Do not _____.
The Seventh Verse 14	Do not commit _____.
The Eighth Verse 15	Do not _____.
The Ninth Verse 16	Do not _____ against your neighbor.
The Tenth Verse 17	Do not _____ anything that is your neighbor's.

▶ Each of the statements below shows one way to break or disobey the Ten Commandments. For each action, write the number of the commandment it breaks. The first answer is given for you.

Third	Saying "God" as part of a curse or insult
	Spending the afternoon wishing that you could have all the presents your friend got for her birthday
	Screaming at a parent or guardian when asked to clean up after dinner
	Taking one of your classmate's pens and not giving it back
	Telling your teacher that your classmates cheated when they really did not
	Valuing what your friends think of you more than what God thinks

48

9-B The Golden Calf

God gave Israel the Law in part to reveal the sin of humanity. As we study what God expects from us, we understand how far we are from His righteousness. No one can keep all the Law of God—it's impossible for anyone but God Himself.

► While God spoke to Moses on Mount Sinai, the people of Israel proved how much they needed God's righteousness. Read **Exodus 32:1–6** and answer the questions below.

⊙ What do the people tell Aaron to do? (v. 1)

_____

_____

⊙ Where does Aaron get the gold needed for the project? (vv. 2–3)

_____

_____

⊙ What does Aaron make with the gold? (v. 4) _____

⊙ What does Aaron say that this object did for Israel? (v. 4)

_____

_____

► Think about everything Aaron did and said in **verse 4**. Which of the Ten Commandments did he break?

_____

So the people worshiped this new idol. As they ate, drank, and danced, they lost all control and began to do terrible things. Even Aaron, Moses' own brother, joined in. After all the signs and miracles Israel had seen, they gave the credit to a fake, shiny cow.

► When God saw what the people did, He was extremely angry. But Moses begged Him not to destroy the people. Read **Exodus 32:11–13**. In your own words, explain why Moses thought that God would not destroy all of Israel.

_____

_____

_____

_____

God told Moses that He would not destroy Israel. But He still judged them, and over 3,000 men died in a single day. Moses lost his temper with the people, and he broke the tablets on which God had written the Law. He rebuked Aaron for letting the people lose control of themselves. All of this proved that the people desperately needed God's help.

9-C The Tabernacle

When God met with Moses on Mount Sinai, He did not just give rules and instructions. He also described a way that Israel could celebrate their relationship with God. The people would make a special place to remind them that God was with them. Here they could worship God and make sacrifices to Him. This place was a tent structure called the *Tabernacle*, and Israel could take it with them wherever they traveled.

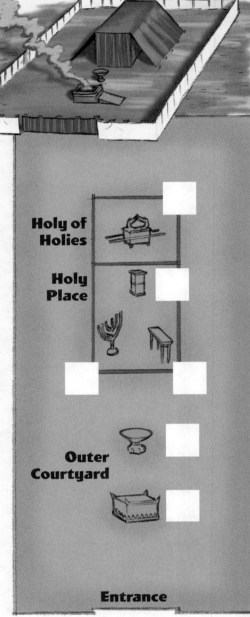

▶ God gave Moses detailed instructions on building the Tabernacle. Read the following description and write the correct **letter** next to each piece of furniture on the map.

- ⊙ When you walk through the single entrance to the courtyard, the first thing you'd see was the **bronze altar** (**A**). Here the Israelites would make burnt offerings and sacrifices.

- ⊙ Just beyond the altar was a **bronze basin** (**B**) or laver, which was used for ritual washing.

- ⊙ The Tabernacle or tent itself had two parts. The Holy Place contained three items: a **golden lampstand** (**C**) with seven candles, a **gold table** (**D**) that held a special kind of bread, and an **altar** (**E**) that burned incense near the back.

- ⊙ The Holy of Holies, the chamber in the far back of the Tabernacle, was hidden by a thick curtain. No one except the high priest ever entered this room, and he entered only one day a year. This was the Day of Atonement, or Yom Kippur, when the high priest offered sacrifices for the sins of the whole nation.

The Holy of Holies contained the **Ark of the Covenant** (**F**), a sacred chest that held items important to Israel's history. These all symbolized God's promises to His people.

Every detail of the Tabernacle helped Israel understand something about God. He expects holiness and respect from His people. And in all these rituals, Christians today can see the foreshadowing of Christ. He was the final sacrifice for our sins—the one who would fulfill God's promises.

▶ Read **Hebrews 4:14–16**. Because Jesus is our high priest today, what can we now do? (v. 16)

_____

_____

_____

_____

Possessing the Land

► God gave Israel the Ten Commandments thousands of years ago, but we should think about how these principles apply to us today.

⊙ What kinds of things could become "gods" in your life?

_____

_____

_____

⊙ It's wrong to use God's name as a curse word. What is another way to show disrespect to Him?

_____

_____

⊙ Most Christians celebrate the Lord's day on Sunday. What are some ways you can keep this day special and focused on God?

_____

_____

_____

_____

⊙ How can you show honor to your parents or guardians even when you disagree with them?

_____

_____

_____

⊙ The Tenth Commandment is one we can break in our mind. What attitudes can help us avoid this sin?

_____

_____

► In **Matthew 5:21–22**, Jesus talks about the Sixth Commandment. In your own words, what does He say about directing your anger at someone?

_____

_____

_____

LESSON 10
Our Holy God

Vocabulary

- **Priest** – A person chosen to perform religious rituals; in Israel, an adult male who helped the people worship God and offer sacrifices

- **Levite** – A person from the tribe of Levi

- **Holy** – Removed from sin or anything unclean; sacred or set apart for God's use

- **Sanctify / Consecrate** – To set apart as holy or sacred

- **Conform** – To become like something or someone; to act like

- **Atone** – To right a wrong

10-A A Picture of God's Holiness

The Book of Leviticus taught Israel's **priests** how to worship God and offer sacrifices to Him. All the Old Testament priests were **Levites**, which is how Leviticus got its name. The book shows us many important things about God.

▶ One such lesson is in **Leviticus 11:45**. How does God describe Himself in this verse?

_____

God wanted His people to be like Him, so He gave them rituals to practice His holiness. Each law was a lesson about the Lawgiver.

▶ Read **Leviticus 20:7-8** and complete the summaries of these commands.

Verse 7	_____ yourselves and be _____, because I am the _____ your God.
Verse 8	Keep My _____ and _____ them. I am the Lord who _____.

God wanted His people to learn holiness. He wants the same for believers today, even though He teaches us in a different way than He taught the Israelites. We do not need to practice the rituals of Leviticus. Instead, we see God's holiness through the life of Jesus.

▶ Read **Romans 12:1-2** and complete the following.

⊙ To worship God today, how should we present or offer ourselves? (v. 1)

_____

_____

⊙ What system should we *not* **conform** to? (v. 2) _____

⊙ Instead, we should be transformed so that we can know and follow the will of _____.

Even though we do not offer animal sacrifices or practice priestly rituals, we should still do right. That means turning away from the sins of the world and following the teachings of Jesus. Only He can truly sanctify us.

▶ Read **1 Peter 1:13–16**. Since Jesus is holy, what should we be? (v. 15)

_____

10-B Instructions for Worship

God chose the Old Testament priests to serve as a go-between for Himself and Israel. The priests helped Israel worship God the way He commanded, and they offered sacrifices on behalf of all the people.

▶ According to **Exodus 28:1**, who did God first choose to be priests?

_____

_____

_____

Like Moses, Aaron was a descendant of Levi, one of Jacob's sons. The Levites became the tribe of priests for Israel. Levite men could spend a few weeks each year working in the Tabernacle or Temple. While serving as priests, they had to follow special rules to honor their Holy God.

► What did the priests do? Read the following verses and briefly describe each duty.

Numbers 1:50	_____ _____ _____
2 Chronicles 30:27	_____ _____ _____ _____
Exodus 24:5	_____ _____ _____

The Sacrificial Offerings

► God taught Israel different sacrifices that they could offer for different reasons. Look up the verses and write the name of the offering described.

Verse	Name of Offering	Description
Leviticus 1:3–4		People could offer this to honor God, but they needed to use a male animal without defects.
Leviticus 2:1–2		This was made of flour and oil, often given as thanks for a harvest.
Leviticus 3:1		People offered this in times of happiness or gratitude, just to praise God. The animal could be male or female.
Leviticus 4:1–3		People offered this to **atone** for doing something evil.
Leviticus 5:15		This was offered when people accidentally did something bad or offended others.

◉ Look up **Exodus 29:45–46**. What did these sacrifices and rituals help Israel remember?

_____

_____

_____

10-C Our Sacrifice and High Priest

When the people of Israel sinned, the priests helped them restore their relationship with God. The people offered sacrifices to show sorrow for their sin. When the fire burned up the sacrifice, their guilt was gone. This pictured God removing their sin.

Today, Christians do not follow these rituals because they are fulfilled in Jesus:

- ◉ **Jesus is our perfect, sinless sacrifice.** He offered Himself to atone for our sins. He died on a cross to take the punishment for all the sins of the whole world.

- ◉ **Jesus is our perfect, sinless priest.** He connects us to God the Father, and we are righteous because of Him.

▶ The Book of Hebrews explains how Jesus served as both Sacrifice and Priest. Look up each verse and fill in the blanks.

Hebrews 2:17	Jesus is a _____ and _____ High Priest.
Hebrews 4:15–16	Jesus faced the same temptations that we do, but He did not _____.
Hebrews 7:23–25	Jesus lives forever, so He holds His _____ always. He also saves people forever.
Hebrews 9:13–14	Jesus' _____ cleanses our conscience so we can serve God.
Hebrews 10:11–14	Jesus offered only _____ sacrifice for sins forever.

Possessing the Land

▶ Think about the passages above and mark the answer to the following questions.

Was Jesus the perfect sacrifice that God required?	☐ Yes	☐ No
Is any sacrifice better than Jesus?	☐ Yes	☐ No
Will anything ever undo the work of Jesus?	☐ Yes	☐ No
Is Jesus the best person to represent us to God the Father?	☐ Yes	☐ No
Can anyone else represent God better than God Himself?	☐ Yes	☐ No
Have you trusted Jesus' sacrifice to atone for your sin?	☐ Yes	☐ No

▶ If you do believe what Jesus taught about His death and resurrection, write a short prayer thanking God for His gift.

_____

_____

_____

_____

_____

_____

_____

_____

Vocabulary

- **Quail** – A kind of bird, somewhat smaller than a chicken

- **Manna** – A kind of food that God gave Israel in the wilderness

- **Leprosy** – In Scripture, a term to describe diseases that could result in sores, loss of feeling, and deformities; used to be incurable

11-A God Provides in the Wilderness

As the Book of Numbers opens, there are millions of Israelite people traveling through the desert toward the land that God has promised them. God has blessed the people so that they've grown in number, despite the hardships they faced.

And just as He promised, God traveled with the people. He instructed Moses to camp all the Israelites by tribe around the Tabernacle. The tribe of Levi divided into four groups closest to the center. All this reminded the people that God lived among them.

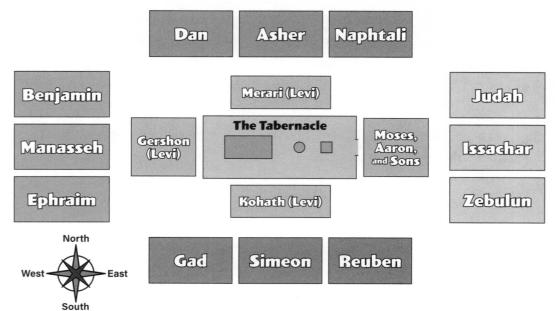

But in the desert, there was little food to eat and almost no water to drink. How were so many people going to survive? They had no need to worry because God would take care of His own.

▶ Read the passages below and complete the chart.

Passage	When Israel Needed . . .	How Did God Provide?
Exodus 15:23–25	Water	He made the water _____.
Exodus 16:11–15, 31	Food	He sent _____ in the evening and a bread-like food that the people called _____.
Exodus 17:3–6	Water	God told Moses to strike a _____, and out came water.
Numbers 20:2–12	Water	God made a _____ pour out water, even though Moses disobeyed Him.
Numbers 21:7–9	Healing from Snake Bites	God told Moses to put a bronze _____ on a pole. Whoever looked at it would be healed.

When the people of Israel needed something, they often let their fear overcome their faith. But God asked the people to trust Him, and He showed them that He would always take care of their needs. Unfortunately, many forgot about His love and complained.

▶ Read **Numbers 12:1–15**, which describes another time the people complained about God.

⊙ Who begins to speak against Moses because they don't like his wife? (v. 1)

_____

⊙ Based on what you read in **verse 2**, what do you think they want?

_____

_____

God had used both of Moses' siblings, but He chose Moses to lead the people. So God stood up for Moses and corrected the other two.

⊙ What happens to Moses' sister? (v. 10)

_____

⊙ What does Moses ask God to do for her? (v. 13) _____

⊙ Does God do what Moses asked? ☐ Yes ☐ No

11-B The First Glimpse of Canaan

God told Moses to count all the people and note the men old enough to join the Israelite army. The people of Israel were getting ready to enter the land that God said He would give them.

▶ To find out what happened next, read **Numbers 13:1–2** and **25–33**. Fill in the blanks below.

God told Moses to send out twelve men

to _____
                    verse 2

Canaan. He picked a man from each tribe.

So the spies traveled all through the land,

and they took some of the fruit to show the

people of Israel. After they returned, they told

Moses what they had seen. They said that the

land flowed with _____ and
                         verse 27

_____! But there were
        verse 27

strong people in Canaan who lived in large,

fortified _____. Most of
                    verse 28

the spies were scared of the Canaanites, but

one named _____ said
                    verse 30

that Israel should go and take the land right

away. The others argued with him, saying that

the Canaanites were much too strong.

▶ Read the following verses from **Numbers 14** and answer the questions.

⊙ **Verses 1–4** – The people are scared. What do they want to do instead of following Moses?

_____

⊙ **Verse 10** – When the people decide to stone Moses and Aaron, who stops them?

_____

⊙ **Verses 26–31** – Because they won't follow God, what does He say will happen to them?

_____

_____

_____

11-C God Blesses Israel

Things looked bad for Israel. What would happen now? Would God still keep His promises? Would they ever reach Canaan? Even though the people had to bear the consequences of their sin, God would not forsake them.

While Israel was living outside of Canaan, King Balak of Moab grew afraid of them. He saw Israel defeat its enemies, and he worried that this new nation would be too strong and too many if they ever attacked him.

▶ Read the following verses from **Numbers 22** and answer the questions.

⊙ **Verses 4–6** – What does King Balak ask the man Balaam to do?

_____

_____

⊙ **Verses 10–12** – What does God tell Balaam *not* to do?

_____

_____

⊙ **Verse 18** – After the king offers Balaam a reward to curse Israel, how does Balaam reply?

_____

_____

▶ Now read **Numbers 22:21–35** and number the events in order from **1** to **5**.

	Balaam finally sees the angel and confesses his sin.
	The donkey sees the angel of the Lord, keeps trying to stop, and finally lies down.
	The angel tells Balaam to speak only what he is told.
	Balaam becomes angry and begins to beat his donkey.
	Balaam saddles his donkey and goes with the Moabites.
	The donkey asks Balaam why he beat her.

▶ Finally, read **Numbers 23:7–12**. The king of Moab wants Balaam to curse the Israelites, but what happens instead?

_____

_____

Possessing the Land

When we forget what God has done for us, we start complaining and grumbling. But God always keeps His promises. We can grow confident in Him by looking at all the promises He has already kept.

▶ What do you tend to complain about?

☐ My food	☐ My clothing	☐ The weather
☐ Schoolwork	☐ Chores	☐ Where I live
☐ My family	☐ My friends	☐ My church

▶ What about these things can you thank God for? Write at least one thing for each item you checked.

_____

_____

_____

_____

_____

_____

_____

_____

Moses' Final Charge

Vocabulary

- **Merciful** – Having mercy; not punishing someone who deserves it; showing an attitude of forgiveness and compassion

12-A Moses Reminds the People

Because the Israelites did not believe God's promise, they did not enjoy the blessings of that promise. Because the people chose not to enter Canaan, they wandered in the desert wilderness for 40 years. Except for Caleb and Joshua, all the adults grew old and died. Only their children saw God's promise fulfilled.

At the end of the 40 years, just before Moses died, he reminded the people of everything God had told them in the Law. This is recorded in the fifth book of the Old Testament, *Deuteronomy*—which means "second law."

God wanted the people to remember the blessings He would give if they believed and obeyed Him—and the bad things that would happen if they did not. So Moses reviewed the history of Israel, from the time they received the Ten Commandments all the way to the present, when they were finally ready to enter Canaan.

► What were Moses' instructions? Read the following verses and fill in the blanks.

Passage	What Moses Taught
Deuteronomy 4:1	Follow these commands so that you can _____ and go in to possess the land that God gives you.
Deuteronomy 4:25–26	If you make any kind of _____ to worship, you will not live long in the land, but instead be destroyed.
Deuteronomy 4:39	Understand that _____ is the only God.
Deuteronomy 6:5	Love God with . . . • All your _____ • All your _____ • All your _____

► Read **Deuteronomy 4:31**. Because God is *merciful*, what three things will He never do to Israel?

1. _____

2. _____

3. _____

Do you remember what covenant this was? You can refresh your memory by looking at page 17. God had already fulfilled some of these promises, and He wanted to give Israel the rest of them. He had so much good waiting for them. To find these blessings, Israel needed to love Him and serve Him alone.

► According to **Deuteronomy 8:2**, what did God accomplish by letting the people wander for 40 years?

_____

_____

_____

_____

_____

12-B The Death of Moses

▶ Moses had lived a long life, but his time was at an end. Read the following passages and choose the correct ending to each sentence.

Numbers 20:7–12 – Back when Moses disobeys God at Meribah, God says . . .

☐ Moses and Aaron will not bring the people into the promised land.	☐ Moses should be executed.	☐ He will abandon the people in the wilderness.

Deuteronomy 3:27–28 – God tells Moses that the next leader of Israel is . . .

☐ Caleb.	☐ Moses' child.	☐ Joshua.

Deuteronomy 34:1–4 – Moses cannot go into Canaan, but God lets him . . .

☐ put one foot into the Jordan River.	☐ cross the Red Sea one more time.	☐ see the land from the top of Mount Nebo.

Deuteronomy 34:10–12 – In tribute to Moses, the end of Deuteronomy says . . .

☐ there was never another prophet like Moses.	☐ that he always did his best.	☐ that the people were happy when he died.

Moses died on Mount Nebo at the age of 120 years. It seems as if God Himself buried Moses in a secret place somewhere on the mountain. This means that the last verses of Deuteronomy must have been written by someone other than Moses—perhaps Joshua.

▶ Read **Hebrews 11:24–29** and answer the following questions about Moses' life.

⊙ How did Moses do all these things mentioned in this passage?

_____

⊙ What did Moses choose to do instead of enjoying the temporary pleasures of sin? (v. 25)

_____

_____

⊙ What did Moses value more than the treasures of Egypt? (v. 26)

_____

_____

⊙ Moses endured because he saw Whom? (v. 27)

_____

12-C Reviewing Israel's Travels

▶ Read the passages below and write the name of the location described. Each location will be used once.

Elim	Kadesh-Barnea	Marah	Mount Nebo	Mount Sinai	Rameses

Location		Passage	What Happened
A.		**Exodus 12:37**	Israel left here right after Passover.
B.		**Exodus 15:23–25**	God made the water here drinkable.
C.		**Exodus 15:27**	The people found 12 springs here.
D.		**Exodus 31:18**	God gave the Law to Moses.
E.		**Deuteronomy 9:23**	Moses sent the 12 spies from here.
F.		**Deuteronomy 34:1**	Moses saw Canaan from here.

▶ Write the **letter** of each location next to the correct dot on the map. Use the clues below.

- ◉ **Location A** is near where the **Nile** flows into the **Mediterranean Sea**.

- ◉ **Location B** is near the northern tip of the **Gulf of Suez**.

- ◉ **Location C** is a little farther southeast down the coast from **B**.

- ◉ **Location D** is on the southern end of the **Sinai Peninsula**, between the **Gulf of Suez** and the **Gulf of Aqaba**.

- ◉ **Location E** is on the southern border of the land of **Canaan**.

- ◉ **Location F** is east of the **Jordan River**.

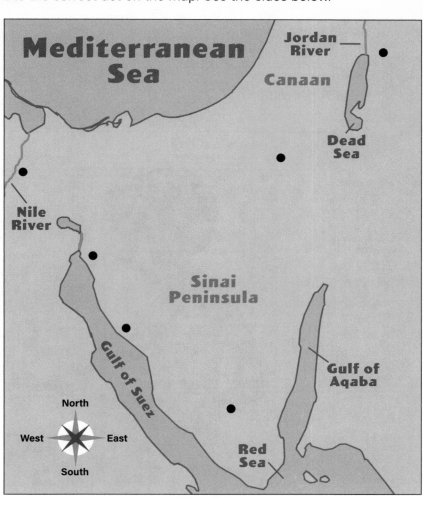

65

Possessing the Land

▶ God told His people to love Him with everything they had. Jesus talked about this command, as well. Read **Matthew 22:34–40** and answer the following questions.

⊙ What question was Jesus asked? (v. 36)

_____

⊙ What was His answer? (vv. 37–38)

_____

_____

⊙ What is the second greatest command? (v. 39)

_____

▶ Jesus said that the whole Law came down to these two commands. For each situation below, name one way that you can show love this week.

⊙ At home: _____

_____

⊙ In your community: _____

_____

⊙ To your church: _____

_____

Vocabulary

- **Generation** – All the people born during the same time period, often 30–40 years

- **Meditate** – To think deeply and continually about something

13-A Israel Gets a New Leader

While the people of Israel traveled through the wilderness, God was preparing someone to lead them into their new home. A new leader would encourage the people to follow their God.

▶ Who was this person? Read the passages below and fill in the blanks.

Exodus 17:9–10	Moses sent a soldier named _____ to fight against _____.
Exodus 24:13–14	Joshua served Moses and went with him up Mount _____. He had been Moses' helper since he was a young man (Num. 11:28).
Numbers 14:6–8	Joshua and Caleb helped spy out the land of Canaan. Unlike the other spies, these two said the Lord would _____ the land to Israel.
Deuteronomy 34:8–9	God told Moses to appoint Joshua as the new leader. After Moses died, Joshua was full of the _____.

Since the time at Kadesh-Barnea when Israel rejected God's promise, Joshua had waited 40 years to enter Canaan. Now Joshua could only lead well if he followed God. This new **generation** of Israelites had great joy and hope. They could not forget the God who guided their parents.

► Read **Joshua 1:1–3** and answer the following questions.

⊙ What does God tell Joshua to do? (v. 2)

_____

_____

⊙ What does God promise to give Joshua and the people? (v. 3)

_____

_____

► Continue reading **Joshua 1:4–9**. Fill in the blanks to summarize how God encouraged Joshua.

	God's Message
Verse 5	I will never _____ you or _____ you.
Verse 6	Be _____ and _____ because you will help the people inherit this land.
Verse 7	Obey the _____ given through Moses.
Verse 8	_____ on this day and night, and you will find success.
Verse 9	Don't be afraid. I will be with you _____ you go.

13-B Crossing the Jordan

► Imagine that you were one of the people about to enter Canaan. Israel had waited centuries for this moment. This nation will finally have a place to call home. How would you feel?

_____

_____

_____

► Read **Joshua 1:10–11**. What does Joshua finally command the people to do?

_____

_____

► Note **verse 11**. How soon will the people cross the Jordan River and enter Canaan?

_____

▶ In the chart below, compare this new generation with their parents. How were they different when standing at Canaan's border?

The First Generation Deuteronomy 1:26–33	The Second Generation Joshua 1:16–18

▶ Read **Joshua 3:9–17**. How did God allow the people to cross the Jordan River?

_____

_____

▶ Finally, read **Joshua 4:1–9**. Why did the people need to bring twelve stones up from the riverbed? (vv. 5–7)

_____

_____

_____

_____

13-C Who Am I?

► Let's review some of the people we've studied so far. Use the following clues to complete the puzzle. If you've forgotten a name, check the given page number.

Across	**Down**
1. I was sold as a slave, but became ruler of Egypt. (p. 34)	**1.** God renamed me "Israel." (p. 25)
3. I was the first man. (p. 10)	**2.** I was the first woman. (p. 10)
6. My father was willing to offer me as a sacrifice to God. (p. 19)	**4.** I was Moses' sister—maybe the one that helped save him as a baby—and I served as a prophetess. (p. 46)
8. I was kind to Abraham's servant and went with him to marry Isaac. (p. 20)	**5.** God promised me that I would father a new nation. (p. 16)
9. I helped lead the Israelites into the promised land. (p. 67)	**7.** God called me to lead the Israelites out of Egypt. (p. 39)
11. Of the twelve spies, only Joshua and I believed that God would give us the land. (p. 59)	**10.** I helped my brother Moses and became one of Israel's first priests. (p. 44)

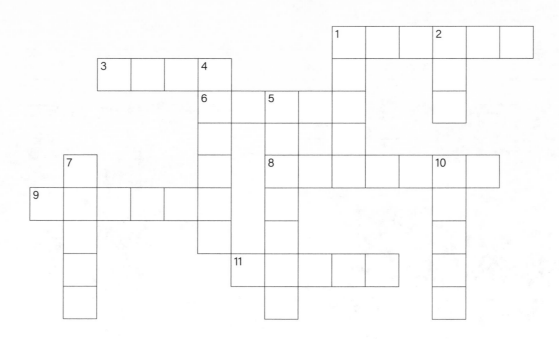

Possessing the Land

► God gives us the courage to do right, and we should encourage other people, as well. For each person below, write one thing that person could be worried about. Then describe one thing you could say or do to encourage them.

Person	Fear or Worry	One Way to Encourage
Your teacher		
A child who lives near you		
An older person in your church		
A police officer		

LESSON 14
Conflict in Canaan

14-A Rahab's Faith

When the people of Israel arrived, Canaan was not empty. It was home to a number of nations. Scripture records that these Canaanites were extremely wicked. They worshiped false gods; they constantly went to war; they mistreated and even killed their children. God had warned them about their sin for hundreds of years, but they continued to reject Him. Now God was going to destroy their power in Canaan and give the land to the Hebrews.

The first stronghold to be conquered was the walled city of Jericho. Joshua prepared for battle by sending two spies to gather information. After the men entered the city, they stayed at the house of a Canaanite woman named Rahab.

▶ Read **Joshua 2:1–21** and mark the correct ending to each sentence.

Verses 2–3: When Jericho's king hears about the spies, he tells Rahab to . . .		
☐ poison them.	☐ bring them out.	☐ ask them if Jericho could make peace with Israel.

Verses 4–7: Instead, Rahab hides the men and tells the king that . . .		
☐ she has never seen any Israelites before.	☐ he can kill them while they sleep that night.	☐ they have already left the city.

Verses 7–11: After men from Jericho leave Rahab, she tells the spies . . .		
☐ to leave and never come back to Jericho again.	☐ that she is secretly an Israelite.	☐ that she knows God has given them the land.

Verses 12–14: Before the spies leave, Rahab asks them to . . .		
☐ spare her family when they conquer the city.	☐ not destroy Jericho.	☐ give her some warning before they attack.

Verses 17–21: The two men instruct Rahab to gather her family and . . .

☐ keep her window open during the attack.	☐ tie a scarlet rope as a signal in her window.	☐ hide in the nearby hills for three days.

▶ Look again at **verses 9–13**. How did Rahab reveal her faith in God?

_____

_____

_____

_____

▶ In your own words, summarize what we can learn about Rahab from **Hebrews 11:31**.

_____

_____

_____

God welcomed Rahab's faith. She was not turned away because of where she was born or what she had done in the past. The Lord showed mercy to her and to every other Canaanite that believed He was God.

14-B Victory at Jericho

▶ Read **Joshua 6:1–25** and answer the following questions.

◉ What does God promise to Joshua? (v. 2)

_____

_____

◉ How many days are the Israelites to march once around the city? (v. 3) _____

◉ What are they supposed to do differently on the seventh day? (vv. 4–5)

_____

_____

◉ What does Joshua tell the people to do on the seventh day? (v. 16)

_____

◉ Who will be spared? (v. 17)

_____

◉ Are the people allowed to take any of Jericho's treasure for themselves? (vv. 18–19)
   ☐ Yes   ☐ No

◉ What does Joshua say would happen if the people disobey this command? (v. 18)

_____

_____

_____

_____

◉ Do the people obey this command? (v. 21)
☐ Yes ☐ No

◉ How does God take care of Rahab and her family? (vv. 22–25)

_____

_____

_____

_____

Because Israel followed God's commands, they were able to take the first city of Canaan without any fighting. They would see victory so long as they obeyed and followed Him. God rewarded each and every step of faith.

14-C Defeat at Ai

The next city ahead of Israel was Ai (pronounced *eye*). This city was strong and fortified, but much smaller than Jericho. The Israelites believed that they could conquer this city as easily as they had Jericho.

▶ Read **Joshua 7:1–12** and match each sentence to its correct ending.

	Verses 4–5: When the Israelites tried to take the city of Ai . . .	**A.** the people destroyed the stolen things.
	Verse 6: Right after Israel was defeated . . .	**B.** they were driven back, and 36 Israelites were killed.
	Verse 11: When Joshua asked what had happened, God told him that . . .	**C.** someone had taken things they were commanded *not* to.
	Verse 12: God said that Israel would not see victory unless . . .	**D.** Joshua tore his clothes, mourned, and humbled himself before God.

► Look back at **Joshua 7:1**. Who stole the things that God forbid? _____

God held the nation of Israel responsible for this sin. This man's sin had to be removed before the people could restore their relationship with God. Achan and his family died because of his disobedience.

► Israel's army went back to Ai—this time with God's blessing. Read **Joshua 8:1–2** and answer the questions below.

⊙ What does God promise Joshua? (v. 1)

_____

_____

⊙ What will God give the people this time? (v. 2)

_____

After Ai, the Israelites went through Canaan and broke the system of power held by the Canaanite kings. Soon it was time for them to settle down and make their home in Canaan.

The people of Israel did not all live in the same place. God told Joshua to divide the land among the twelve tribes. The nation of Israel spread throughout Canaan, claiming what God had promised them.

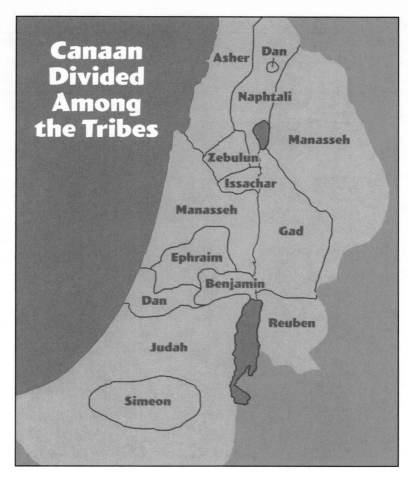

Possessing the Land

▶ Read **Joshua 24:17–18.** The Israelites remembered the things God had done for them. Make your own list of three things God has done for you in the past year.

- He led me to this school

- He answered my prairs

- He helped me win baseball championship

▶ By the time Joshua died, the people of Israel possessed much of the land of Canaan. They made a commitment again to the Lord. According to **Joshua 24:24**, what was this commitment?

They will obey and serve god.

▶ Choose one of the blessings or privileges that you listed above. How can you honor God with this blessing?

He led me here and I really enjoy this school

Judging Israel

Vocabulary

- **Judge (noun)** – In the Old Testament, a leader chosen by God to save Israel from its enemies

- **Judge (verb)** – To declare something right or wrong; to decide what is just and fair

- **Repent** – To regret sin and turn back toward God; to ask God to forgive you

15-A Turning Away from God

The Israelites finally settled into the land that God had promised them. God had proved Himself faithful, and the people were enjoying His blessings. But there was a big problem—the people refused to obey a very important command.

▶ Read **Numbers 33:51–52**. What does God tell the Israelites to do when they enter Canaan?

_____

_____

_____

▶ Read **Joshua 23:12–13**. What does Joshua say will happen if the Israelites instead ally with the Canaanite nations?

_____

_____

_____

At the start of the Book of Judges, we read that Israel did not completely drive out the Canaanites from the land. Several of the tribes of Israel chose to live among the Canaanites. Before too long, some of the Israelites worshiped false Canaanite gods instead of the one true God.

▶ Read the following verses from **Judges 2** and fill in the blanks.

Verses 1–3	The angel condemned Israel because they didn't tear down the _____ of the Canaanites. The false gods would become like a snare or trap to Israel.
Verses 8–10	_____ died at the age of 110 years. After his generation passed away, there was a new generation that did not remember what God had done.
Verses 12–13	The people of Israel soon _____ the Lord and instead worshiped false gods like Ba'al and Ashtaroth.
Verse 15	Because of this, the hand of the Lord was _____ them. They could not win against their enemies, and they suffered greatly.
Verse 16	So God raised up _____ to save the people from their enemies.
Verse 17	But the people did not _____ to these leaders and soon worshiped other gods once again.

▶ Note **Judges 2:18**. How did God respond when the people suffered and cried out?

_____

▶ But look at **verse 20**. How did God respond when the people forgot Him and went back to sin?

_____

Sadly, this cycle happened over and over again. The people turned away from God and worshiped false gods instead. So God allowed them to suffer in order to get their attention and bring them back to Himself. The people **repented** for a little while, but soon they went right back to sinning again.

Turning from God ➡ Suffering ➡ Repentance ➡ Deliverance

▶ Finally, read **Judges 21:25**, the very last verse of the book. How does the writer sum up the people's problem?

_____

_____

_____

15-B Deborah the Judge

Even though the people kept rejecting God and forgetting Him, the Lord never left His people or broke His promises. He loved them and cared about them deeply, so He sent judges to help save the people and turn them back toward God. The Book of Judges tells us about twelve of these leaders, and one of them was a woman named Deborah.

▶ Read Deborah's story in **Judges 4:1–24**. Note what each of the people below did in this passage.

Barak	Deborah	Jabin	Jael	Sisera
A leader in Israel's army	A prophetess and judge who led Israel	A Canaanite king who oppressed Israel	A Kenite woman	The leader of Jabin's army

▶ Read each statement below and write the name of the person described. Some of the names above will be used more than once.

	I let Sisera hide in my tent—for a while, at least.
	I told Barak that God said to fight Jabin's army with 10,000 men.
	I led 900 iron chariots, which I used to frighten the Israelites.
	I settled disagreements for Israel and gave them God's word.
	I did not want to battle Sisera unless Deborah went with me.
	I killed Sisera and then showed Barak what I had done.
	After my army was defeated, the Israelites came to destroy me.
	I led the Israelites in pursuit of Sisera.

After the battle, Deborah and Barak celebrated by singing a song together. It was a song of praise to God for what He had done. You can find what they sang in Judges 5.

▶ For now, just look at **Judges 5:31**. How did they describe those who love God?

_____

▶ What do you think this means?

_____

_____

_____

15-C Gideon the Judge

▶ God called an unlikely man to serve as a judge. Read **Judges 6:1-16** and fill in the blanks to complete the story.

Because Israel turned toward evil, God allowed them to suffer under the rule of

_____. It became so bad that the Israelites needed to hide in
                verse 1

caves and strongholds. Whenever the Israelites tried to farm, the Midianites and Amalekites

would destroy the _____ of the land. Humbled by Midian, the
                              verse 4

people of Israel finally _____ to the Lord for help.
                              verse 6

A man named _____ was working in secret to hide his wheat
                      verse 11

from the Midianites. The angel of the Lord appeared and said that the Lord was with him.

The angel called Gideon a _____.
                                                  verse 12

Gideon asked the angel why God let all these things happen, if He truly was with Israel.

Gideon said that the Lord had _____ them and given them over
                                        verse 13

to Midian. But the Lord told Gideon to go in strength and _____ Israel.
                                                                verse 14

Gideon wondered how he could save Israel. His family was the weakest in the tribe of

Manasseh, and he was the _____ in his house. But the Lord
                                      verse 15

said that He would be _____ Gideon, who would defeat Midian.
                            verse 16

Gideon needed a lot of encouragement, but he eventually obeyed God. He gathered a large number of soldiers to battle against Midian.

▶ But note **Judges 7:2**. What did God say about Gideon's army?

_____

⊙ What would happen if God let Israel win with such an army?

_____

_____

⊙ So according to **Judges 7:8**, God trimmed Gideon's army until there were only _____ men left.

⊙ How does **Judges 7:12** describe the enemy army?

_____

_____

▶ Finally, read **Judges 7:19–22** and answer the following.

⊙ Who wins the battle? _____

⊙ Does Israel need to attack the enemy camp? ☐ Yes ☐ No

Possessing the Land

▶ Unfortunately, Israel's victory did not last long. Read **Judges 8:33** and explain why not.

_____

_____

_____

▶ What right things do you often forget to do?

_____

_____

_____

▶ List at least one way you can remind yourself to do right.

_____

_____

_____

_____

LESSON 16
The Story of Ruth

Vocabulary

- **Glean** – To gather crops by hand, sometimes after the main harvest is over

- **Compassion** – Showing love and gentleness to someone who needs it

- **Redeemer** – A person that *redeems*; someone who can rightfully claim and take something

- **Threshing Floor** – A wide, flat place where workers separate grain from the rest of the plant

16-A Ruth Cares for Naomi

Ruth lived during the time described in the Book of Judges. Many of the Israelites worshiped false gods and did wicked things, but there were still a few who followed and obeyed the one true God.

Naomi and her family left the promised land because of a famine. There was not enough food in Israel, so they traveled to Moab and settled there. But soon, tragedy struck.

▶ Read **Ruth 1:3–9** and answer the following questions.

⊙ What happens to Naomi's husband Elimelech? (v. 3) _____

⊙ Who marries Naomi's two sons? (vv. 3–4)

_____

⊙ Then what happens to Naomi's sons? (v. 5) _____

⊙ When Naomi hears that there is food in Israel, what does she decide to do? (vv. 6–7)

_____

Naomi told her two daughters-in-law to go back to their own families. There was nothing for them to gain by staying with her. She hoped God would bless them like they had blessed their husbands. So Orpah did what Naomi said and left—but Ruth did not.

► Look ahead to **Ruth 1:14–18** and answer the following.

⊙ In your own words, how does Ruth respond when Naomi tells her to go away? (vv. 16–17)

_____

_____

⊙ Why do you think Ruth says this? What do you think she is feeling?

_____

_____

► Naomi and Ruth traveled to Bethlehem, where they settled down to make a new life after the death of their husbands. Read **Ruth 1:19–22** and **2:1–3**. Think about what it might be like for an outsider to move to Israel. Describe at least one difficulty Ruth would face.

_____

_____

_____

_____

_____

16-B Ruth Finds a Redeemer

► To find out how God provided for Ruth and Naomi, continue reading in **Ruth 2:1–16**. Then mark the correct ending to the following sentences.

Verse 2: Ruth decides to help her mother-in-law by . . .		
☐ going to **glean** in the field of someone who would let her.	☐ becoming a blacksmith.	☐ planting and **gleaning** her own crops.

Verses 1–3: Ruth happens to work in a place owned by . . .		
☐ a judge of Israel.	☐ a relative of Elimelech.	☐ Naomi's sister.

Verses 5–7: When Boaz asks who Ruth is, the young man tells him that . . .		
☐ she is Boaz's future wife, of course.	☐ she might be Naomi's slave.	☐ she is a Moabite who came back with Naomi.

Verses 8–9: Boaz shows compassion by encouraging Ruth to . . .		
☐ gather and rest with Boaz's workers.	☐ take anything she wanted from his house.	☐ find something easier to do.

Verses 10–12: When Ruth asks Boaz why he was so kind, he says that . . .		
☐ he was lonely and wanted to get Ruth's attention.	☐ he heard how kind Ruth was to Naomi, and he hoped that God would repay her.	☐ he had committed a terrible sin many years ago, and he wanted to atone for it.

When Naomi heard about Boaz, she praised God for His kindness. Naomi explained to Ruth that Boaz was a close relative of Elimelech. It seemed like God had guided these people together.

Some time later, Naomi encouraged Ruth to ask Boaz to be her **redeemer**. This meant that Boaz would marry Ruth and carry on Elimelech's family name. Naomi explained how Ruth should ask Boaz.

▶ Read **Ruth 3:1–3**. Where did Naomi say to meet Boaz?

_____

▶ Note **Ruth 3:9–11**. Ruth followed Naomi's instructions and talked with Boaz. Basically, she asked him to marry her. Did he agree?　☐ Yes　☐ No

There was one problem. Before Boaz could marry Ruth, there was a closer relative of Elimelech who needed to give up his rights. So the next day, Boaz went to the town gate. This was where the people of the city made important legal decisions—much like a court.

Boaz met the other relative and explained what was going on. At first, the closer relative wanted to be the redeemer for Elimelech's family. He would be able to get some of Elimelech's old land. But Boaz explained that to redeem the land, the redeemer would also need to marry Ruth, a Moabite.

▶ Look at **Ruth 4:6**. What did the closer relative say after he heard that?

_____

_____

After the closer relative gave up his right, Israel's customs allowed Boaz and Ruth to marry. In the end, God guided them together and blessed their love for each other.

16-C The Redeemer of the World

▶ Before too long, Boaz and Ruth had a son together. Read **Ruth 4:13–17** and answer the questions below.

     ◉ Naomi has been through a lot of hardship, but life is starting to seem better. How do her friends encourage her? (vv. 14–15)

     _____

     _____

     _____

     ◉ Who is born into this new family? Use **verses 17** and **22** to complete the chart below.

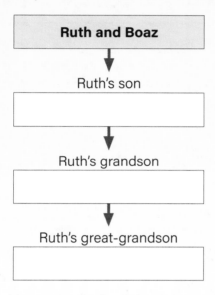

     You might recognize that last name. Ruth and Boaz were the great-grandparents of Israel's most famous shepherd.

▶ Look in the New Testament at **Matthew 1:1**. Many years later, who was born in the line of David?

_____

▶ Because of this family, we can be redeemed, too. Read **Galatians 3:10–14** and fill in the blanks.

Verse 10	Anyone trusting in the Law for righteousness is under a _____.
Verse 11	Instead, the _____ live by _____.
Verse 13	Christ redeemed us from this curse by becoming a _____ for us. This is what happened when He died on the cross.
Verse 14	Through Jesus Christ, the blessing of _____ was fulfilled.

▶ What did Jesus redeem us from?

_____

_____

▶ What did Jesus do to pay for our redemption?

_____

_____

Possessing the Land

▶ How does God describe Himself in **Exodus 34:6**?

_____

_____

_____

Ruth and Boaz both showed compassion because they followed God. They cared for the people around them. They wanted to be part of God's plan to bless others. When they saw people in need, they saw a chance for God to work.

▶ How can you show compassion to those who are suffering? For each situation below, mark the response that *best* shows compassion.

Situation	Response
Your little sister is crying because she's hungry, but your parent is busy helping another sibling.	☐ Pretend you don't hear her. ☐ Help her get a snack. ☐ Laugh at her.
A boy trips and falls, dropping his lunch on the floor.	☐ Join everyone else in making fun of him. ☐ Offer to share your lunch with him. ☐ Take a picture of him to share with others.
A family you know had their house burn down.	☐ Tell your friends how sad it is. ☐ Ask them why they let their house burn down. ☐ Help others collect food and clothes they need.
A classmate is having trouble during a test and asks to see your answers.	☐ Show her what you wrote on the test. ☐ Give her the wrong answers on purpose. ☐ Say no, but offer to help her study next time.

LESSON 17
Review

17-A Who's Who?

► Match each description to the correct person. If you forget, check the given page number.

	1. The first man created by God (p. 10)	**A.** Abraham
	2. A judge who rescued Israel with Barak (p. 79)	**B.** Ruth
	3. Killed his brother when God did not accept a sacrifice (p. 13)	**C.** Cain
	4. Created the world and will one day reveal Himself to all (p. 7)	**D.** Deborah
	5. Promised by God that he would father a great nation (p. 17)	**E.** Eve
	6. Called by God to lead the Hebrews out of Egypt (p. 39)	**F.** Gideon
	7. Obeyed God's command to sacrifice a lamb, but was killed by his brother (p. 13)	**G.** God
	8. The first to eat the fruit that God said not to eat (p. 11)	**H.** Abel
	9. God's chosen Messiah, the Redeemer for the world (pp. 85–86)	**I.** Isaac
	10. Sold as a slave, but later saved his family from a famine (p. 34)	**J.** Jesus
	11. Chosen by God to be a priest with his sons (p. 53)	**K.** Jacob
	12. He led the Hebrews into Canaan (p. 68)	**L.** Joseph
	13. Led 300 men to help save Israel from Midian (p. 81)	**M.** Moses
	14. Disobeyed God by keeping treasures from Jericho (p. 75)	**N.** Achan
	15. Tricked his father into blessing him instead of Esau (p. 22)	**O.** Adam
	16. Moved to Israel while taking care of her mother-in-law (p. 83)	**P.** Aaron
	17. Helped two Israelite spies and was saved by her faith (p. 73)	**Q.** Joshua
	18. Traveled with her husband to Canaan, where she gave birth to her firstborn son at the age of 90 (pp. 18–19)	**R.** Rahab
	19. The son that God promised to Abraham and Sarah (p. 19)	**S.** Sarah

17-B Names and Places

► Look at the definitions on the next page and write the correct vocabulary words in the puzzle below. If you forget a word, check the given page number.

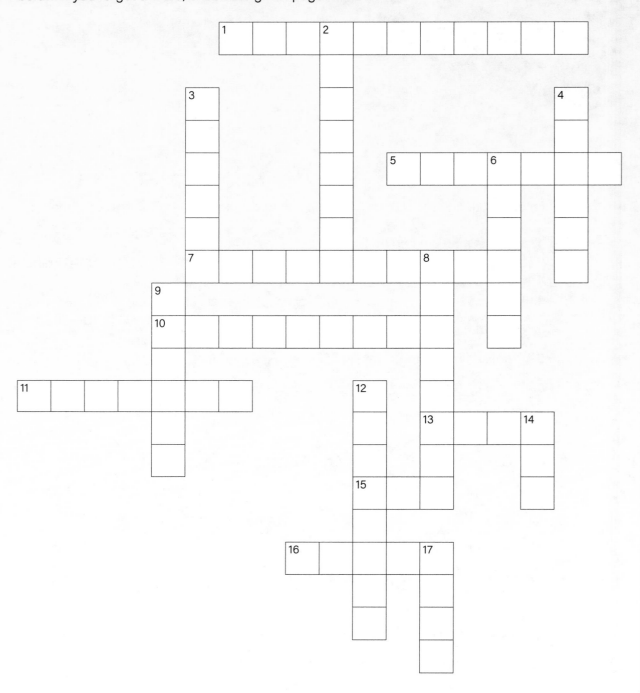

Across

1. The way God worked through human writers to record Scripture; "God-breathed" (p. 5)

5. A king or queen of Egypt; often claimed to be a god (p. 26)

7. In Scripture, a tent compound where God showed His presence to Israel (p. 47)

10. To give up something, often to serve or worship God (p. 16)

11. The seventh day of the week; means "rest;" the day God rested after creating the world (p. 47)

13. A statue or image of a false god; often worshiped (p. 41)

15. The decision to break God's law; turning away from God (p. 10)

16. A belief in something we cannot see or prove; trust in God (p. 16)

Down

2. A Jewish holiday celebrating the day God rescued the Israelites from Egypt (p. 41)

3. To regret sin and turn back toward God; to ask God to forgive you (p. 77)

4. Leaving or departing a place; Israel's departure from Egypt (p. 41)

6. To buy back what was lost (p. 10)

8. Everything God brought into being; the universe (p. 10)

9. The name given to Jacob and his descendants; means "wrestling with God" (p. 21)

12. Giving someone special favor or grace; words that wish happiness or success (p. 21)

14. A rule that shows how to apply a moral idea or principle (p. 47)

17. Removed from sin or anything unclean; sacred or lifted up (p. 52)

► Write the name of each place marked on the map below. Write the correct name next to the matching letter. If you need help, look at the maps on pages 45 and 65.

A. The _____ Sea

B. The _____ River

C. The land of _____

D. The _____ Sea

E. The land of _____

F. The _____ River

G. The possible place of Mount _____

H. The _____ Sea

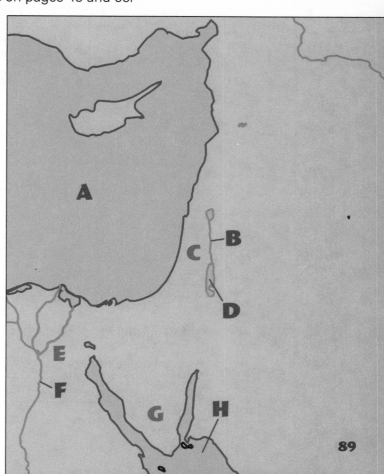

17-C God's Promises

God's Promises to Humanity

▶ Think back to the lesson from the Book of Genesis, and answer the following questions.

◉ God told Adam and Eve that they would die if they disobeyed. In **Genesis 3:4–5**, What did the serpent tell Eve instead?

_____

_____

◉ List two results of the first sin. Note page 12.

_____

_____

_____

_____

◉ Who fulfilled God's promise in **Genesis 3:15**? Note page 14.

_____

God's Promises to Israel

▶ Fill in the blanks below.

A **covenant** is a _____ between two or more

people (p. 16). In Genesis 12, God made a covenant with _____ (p. 17).

God promised . . .

    ◉ To show this man a _____

    ◉ To make from him a great _____

    ◉ To _____ those who blessed him

    ◉ And to _____ those who cursed him

God also promised that through this man's descendants, all the peoples of the earth would

be _____. God fulfilled all these promises by . . .

    ◉ Multiplying the people while they were in _____ (p. 36)

    ◉ Leading them through the wilderness to the land of _____ (p. 68)

    ◉ Sending _____, a descendant of David, to redeem us (p. 85)

L E S S O N   1 8
The Last Judge of Israel

Vocabulary

- **Vow** – A serious, unbreakable promise, sometimes to God Himself

18-A Samuel Serves God

As the time of judges came to an end, God chose a special leader named Samuel. This man was a priest who had served God since he was a child. Some people call Samuel the last true judge of Israel.

▶ Before Samuel was born, his mother Hannah could not have a child for a long time. Read about her struggle in **1 Samuel 1:9–17** and **24–28**. Then mark the correct ending to the following sentences.

Verses 9–10: Hannah is sad that she could not have a son, so she . . .

| ☐ complains every day to her husband. | ☐ prays to God. | ☐ decides that children are terrible. |

Verse 11: Hannah vows that if God gives her a son, she will . . .

| ☐ celebrate with a feast. | ☐ never cut her hair again. | ☐ offer him back to God. |

Verse 17: Eli thinks she is drunk, but when he realizes she is praying . . .

| ☐ he says he hopes that God will give her what she asked. | ☐ he thinks she is being silly. | ☐ he walks away without saying anything. |

Verses 24–25: When Samuel is old enough, Hannah brings him to . . .

| ☐ Eli. | ☐ Elkanah. | ☐ David. |

As a child, Samuel helped Eli at the Tabernacle. The boy learned how priests could help people connect with God. And before long, Samuel himself heard from God.

▶ Read **1 Samuel 3:1–18** and then answer the following questions.

⊙ At first, who does Samuel think is calling him? (vv. 4–5)

_____

⊙ After Eli realizes what is happening, what does the priest tell Samuel to do? (v. 9)

_____

_____

_____

⊙ The Lord treats the boy like a prophet and gives him a message about Eli. Is this message good news? (vv. 12–14)
☐ Yes ☐ No

▶ In the morning, Eli told Samuel to explain what God had said. How would you feel if you needed to deliver that message?

_____

_____

Eli had allowed his sons to keep dishonoring God at the Tabernacle. The people of Israel could not count on Eli's family to speak for God. So in Eli's place, Samuel became a voice for truth. As the boy grew into a man, God spoke through him.

18-B Israel Wants a King

During this time, Israel continued to have trouble with their neighboring nations. Perhaps their biggest enemy was the Philistines. In 1 Samuel 4, the Philistine army defeated the Israelites in battle and captured the Ark of the Covenant.

But God did not allow these enemies to keep His ark. Wherever the Philistines took it, there was trouble, sickness, and misery. God had cursed those who dishonored Him. Eventually, the Philistines brought the ark back to Israel with an apology.

▶ After the death of Eli, Samuel served as a judge for Israel. Read **1 Samuel 7:3–11** and answer the following questions.

⊙ What does Samuel first tell the people to do? (vv. 3–4)

_____

_____

◉ What does Samuel do when the Philistines come to attack the people at Mizpah? (vv. 8–9)

_____

_____

◉ How does God protect Israel? (vv. 10–11)

_____

_____

Samuel was a good leader because he trusted God and encouraged the people to do right. But over time, the Israelites demanded something different.

▶ Read **1 Samuel 8:1–9** and fill in the blanks.

Verse 1	When he is old, Samuel chooses his _____ to lead and judge Israel. Their names are Joel and Abijah.
Verse 3	The two sons do not _____ in Samuel's ways. Instead of being good judges, they take bribes and twist justice.
Verses 4–5	So the leaders of Israel tell Samuel to choose a _____ to lead them, just like the rest of the nations have.
Verses 6–7	When Samuel prays, _____ tells him to listen to the people. They are not rejecting Samuel, but are instead rejecting God and His rule.
Verse 9	God tells Samuel to explain what a _____ will be like.

Samuel warned the people about what would happen if they wanted another ruler besides God. A king would take away . . .

- ◉ Their sons to fight, to farm, and to make weapons
- ◉ Their daughters to make food and other goods
- ◉ The best of their crops
- ◉ A tenth of all their grain, vineyards, and flocks
- ◉ Many of their servants and animals to do his own work

▶ Continue reading **1 Samuel 8:17–22** and complete the following.

◉ Finally, Samuel says that they will be the king's _____. (v. 17)

◉ If they cry out when that happens, God will not _____ them. (v. 18)

◉ Do the people care about Samuel's warning? (v. 19) ☐ Yes ☐ No

◉ Does God allow the people to have their king? (v. 22) ☐ Yes ☐ No

18-C Talking with God

Listening to God

Some people today wish they could hear God's voice just like Samuel could. But God does speak to us. He uses many different ways to teach us truth.

▶ How does God teach us? Read each passage below and complete the chart.

Passage	Who or What Does God Use?	How Does God Use Them?
Psalm 19:1–4		They show the _____ of God (v. 1).
Proverbs 1:8–9		They can instruct and teach us.
Ephesians 4:11–13	Apostles, prophets, evangelists, pastors, and teachers	They can _____ us for the work of serving (v. 12).
2 Timothy 3:14–17		It prepares us for every kind of good _____. (v. 17)

◉ Which of the tools above do you think is most important? Why?

_____

_____

_____

Speaking to God

Prayer is spending time with God and talking to Him. Since God is everywhere and knows everything, you don't have to speak loudly or perform a complicated ritual. He hears even our thoughts, so we can speak with Him in many ways.

When we pray, we can . . .

- ◉ **Worship God**—Praising Him for what He's like and what He's done
- ◉ **Thank God**—Blessing Him for His goodness
- ◉ **Confess to God**—Asking Him to show us our sins and remove them
- ◉ **Depend on God**—Telling Him what we need and want

Prayer helps build your relationship with God. It's a special thing just between you and Him. Prayer is *not* . . .

- ⦿ A way to show off to other people
- ⦿ A ritual to keep bad things from happening to us
- ⦿ A spell or formula to make God do what we want

Possessing the Land

► How much time do you spend talking with God? Mark each statement from **1** (rarely) to **5** (often).

	Rarely		Sometimes		Often
I read my Bible carefully.	1	2	3	4	5
I pay attention to what I hear in my church.	1	2	3	4	5
I spend time thinking about what I learn in Bible class.	1	2	3	4	5
I do my schoolwork with a desire to learn God's truth.	1	2	3	4	5
I thank God for what He's done for me.	1	2	3	4	5
I tell God about what I need and hope.	1	2	3	4	5
I talk to others about what I learn from the Bible.	1	2	3	4	5

► Describe one way you can listen better to God's truth.

_____

_____

LESSON 19
The First King of Israel

Vocabulary

- **Anoint** – To put oil on someone; shows that the person is chosen for a special purpose

- **Siege** – Surrounding an enemy location, cutting off its supplies, and attacking it

- **Spoil / Plunder** – Goods and treasures taken by force from an enemy

19-A God Chooses Saul

The people of Israel ignored God's warnings and demanded a king. Though God warned the people about human kings, He gave them one anyway. God showed Samuel a young man from the tribe of Benjamin. This Benjamite was named Saul, and he became Israel's first king. God used him to save Israel from enemy attacks.

► Note how Saul is described in **1 Samuel 9:1–2**. Draw a picture of him below.

► When Samuel **anointed** Saul, he gave him a very specific command. Read **1 Samuel 10:8**. What did Saul need to do when he went to worship in Gilgal?

wait 7 days until he tells him what to do.

Even though Saul was king, God still spoke through Samuel. A king could help protect Israel, but the people needed to respect God first of all.

Samuel announced to everyone that God had chosen a king for Israel, but not everyone was impressed with Saul. Some Israelites didn't think this young man could protect them.

► In Saul's early years as king, what kind of decisions did he make? Read the following passages and answer the questions.

Situation	Saul's Response
The Ammonites put the Israelite city of Jabesh under **siege**. So Saul gathered an army. The Israelites defended their people against the Ammonites.	**1 Samuel 11:11–15** – Who does Saul praise for the victory? (v. 13) _God_
The Philistines were about to attack Israel. Saul waited in Gilgal for Samuel to make sacrifices, like always. But the Israelites were afraid, and some began to run away. Where was Samuel?	**1 Samuel 13:8–14** – How does Saul disobey God? (vv. 13–14) _He did not give god the burnt offering_
It took a long time to defeat the Philistines. Saul was impatient, and he only had 600 soldiers to follow him.	**1 Samuel 14:23–26** – What does Saul tell his soldiers not to do until after the battle? (v. 24) _Eat the food._
After God gave Israel victory over the Philistines, Saul wanted to know if he could chase the enemy into their own lands.	**1 Samuel 14:35–37** – When Saul asks God if He will give Israel victory again, does God answer him? ☐ Yes ☒ No

► What could Saul have done to be a better leader?

He could of not disobeyed god and he could be honest.

19-B Saul Disobeys God

Even though God blessed King Saul, the man let his disobedience become a habit. He had a great deal of power, so he thought he could ignore Samuel's instructions. Saul made up his own rules and sacrificed the way he wanted. He didn't understand that God values the *attitude* of worship more than the *acts* of worship.

► Because the Amalekites attacked God's people, God told Saul to the destroy the Amalekites completely. Read the following verses from **1 Samuel 15** and fill in the blanks.

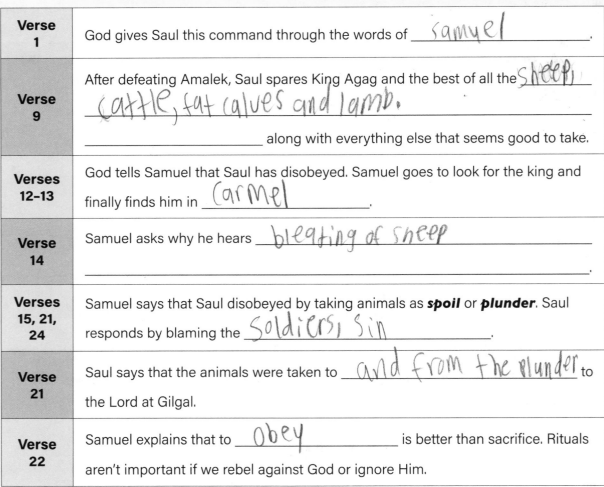

Verse 1	God gives Saul this command through the words of ___Samuel___.
Verse 9	After defeating Amalek, Saul spares King Agag and the best of all the ___Sheep, cattle, fat calves and lamb.___ _____ along with everything else that seems good to take.
Verses 12–13	God tells Samuel that Saul has disobeyed. Samuel goes to look for the king and finally finds him in ___Carmel___.
Verse 14	Samuel asks why he hears ___bleating of sheep___ .
Verses 15, 21, 24	Samuel says that Saul disobeyed by taking animals as **spoil** or **plunder**. Saul responds by blaming the ___soldiers, Sin___.
Verse 21	Saul says that the animals were taken to ___and from the plunder___ to the Lord at Gilgal.
Verse 22	Samuel explains that to ___Obey___ is better than sacrifice. Rituals aren't important if we rebel against God or ignore Him.

► Imagine you are Samuel and you know that King Saul has stopped following God. How would you pray to God during this time? What would you ask for?

___I would pray and ask for God to forgive saul.___

19-C Obedience Is Better than Sacrifice

▶ Saul thought it was better to sacrifice the Amalekites' animals instead of destroying them, as God commanded. Continue reading **1 Samuel 15:22–31** and answer the following questions.

⊙ Again, what does God enjoy more than sacrifices? (v. 22)

obey

⊙ What is rebellion like? (v. 23)

Sin of divination evil of idolatry.

⊙ Because Saul rejects the word of the Lord, what does God do? (v. 23)

Rejects him of King

⊙ Note Saul's apology in **verses 24–25** and **30–31**. Do you think the king was sorry for his sin? Why or why not?

Yes because God let him worship Him.

Possessing the Land

▶ Read the following story.

Grayson rolled back and forth in his bed, when suddenly he realized what day it was. He looked at his clock—9:15 already?! He'd be late for church. He threw on his clothes and ran to the kitchen to grab something for breakfast.

His little sister was already there. "Would you get me the oatmeal?" she asked him, pointing to the top shelf. "I can't reach it."

"Ask Dad," Grayson replied. "I have to hurry."

When Grayson got to church, he flew past Mrs. Jacobs. She had dropped her Bible and was poking at it with her cane.

Grayson thought, *Someone else will help her. I can't, or I'll be late again.*

He reached the door of his class just as the teacher began to speak. There was another boy standing just outside in the hall. Grayson didn't recognize him—he must be a visitor.

The boy saw Grayson and spoke up. "Hi, is this the middle school class? I'm not sure where to go."

Grayson didn't have time. Pretending not to hear, he sped through the door and landed hard in his seat at the back of the classroom. The teacher didn't say anything about it.

Grayson felt pretty good, so he took a moment to congratulate himself. *That was a rough morning, but I got to church. That's all God can ask of me, right? He wanted me here to learn about Him, and He helped me move fast.*

Thoughts like these kept Grayson happy as the teacher continued saying whatever it was she said.

▶ Read **Matthew 22:34–40** again, or review what you wrote on page 66. Do you think that Grayson obeyed these commands? ☐ Yes ☐ No

▶ How was Grayson like King Saul?

_____

_____

_____

▶ Imagine you are Grayson's parent, and he tells you all about his morning. He's very proud of himself. What would you tell him? What advice would you give him for next Sunday?

_____

_____

_____

_____

_____

Instead of obeying God, sometimes we just try to *look* obedient. Like Saul, we worry too much about what the people around us think. We let our pride control us.

Take a moment and ask God to show you any ways that you've disobeyed Him this past week. Then ask Him to help you follow Him better.

20-A Israel's New Hero

Another Anointing

God told Samuel that He had chosen a new king from the sons of a man named Jesse, who lived in Bethlehem. Samuel needed to go and anoint the person God revealed. So Samuel went to Jesse and invited all his sons to offer a sacrifice with him.

► Read **1 Samuel 16:6–13** and answer the following questions.

⊙ What does Samuel think of Eliab, Jesse's oldest son? (v. 6)

_____

⊙ In your own words, explain how God sees differently than humans can. (v. 7)

_____

_____

_____

⊙ Which son does God finally choose? (vv. 11–13) _____

⊙ Besides the anointing, how does God show His approval for this boy? (v. 13)

_____

David Trusts God

David had been chosen by God to be the next king of Israel, but it was not yet time for him to replace Saul. In the meantime, God prepared David. At home, the boy was still a shepherd, but sometimes he served King Saul as a musician or armor-bearer. David saw that the king no longer had God's blessing. But the boy never once did anything to harm Saul or claim the throne for himself. It seems David trusted God to fulfill His plan in His own way, in His own timing.

▶ During this time, the Israelites were at war with the Philistines. Read **1 Samuel 17:20–51** and number the events in order from **1** to **10**. The first is marked for you.

	David volunteers to fight Goliath.
	David hears the gigantic Philistine Goliath defy the Israelites and their God.
	When the Philistines see that their champion is dead, they turn and run.
	David knocks Goliath down with one shot from a sling.
1	David leaves his flocks to bring supplies to his brothers on the battlefield.
	Saul says that David is too young and unskilled to fight Goliath.
	David says that God protected him from lions and bears. He can defeat Goliath.
	David prepares to fight Goliath with only a sling and five stones.
	Goliath mocks and curses David.
	Eliab accuses David of leaving his sheep just to watch the battle.

▶ Note **verses 46–47** again. Who does David praise for the victory? _____

▶ Who showed more trust in God: David or Saul? Explain your answer.

_____

_____

_____

_____

20-B Saul Envies David

A New Enemy

After the defeat of Goliath, Saul made David a commander in his army. This shepherd succeeded wherever Saul sent him. When the Israelite soldiers finally returned home from fighting, all of Israel celebrated their victory. There was singing and dancing, and everyone knew the story of David and Goliath.

▶ Read **1 Samuel 18:7–9**. What song angered Saul?

_____

_____

_____

▶ Read ahead in **1 Samuel 18:12–16**. Why was Saul afraid of David?

_____

_____

▶ Very soon, Saul hated David—so much that he even tried to kill David. Read the following passages and describe what Saul tried to do.

Passage	What Saul Tried to Do
1 Samuel 18:17	
1 Samuel 18:10–11 **1 Samuel 19:9–10**	
1 Samuel 19:15	

A New Friend

Shortly after David killed Goliath, he met Jonathan, the son of King Saul. Jonathan and David became fast friends. Jonathan cared for David as much as Saul hated David.

This friendship was unusual. Jonathan was in line to become king after his father died. Jonathan also knew that David was anointed as king. But instead of becoming rivals, Jonathan and David defended each other. They both understood Saul's problems, and they both trusted God to do what was best for Israel.

► Match each passage to what it reveals about Jonathan and David.

A. 1 Samuel 18:1	B. 1 Samuel 19:1–2	C. 1 Samuel 19:4–5	D. 1 Samuel 20:12–16	E. 2 Samuel 9:1–7

	Jonathan and David were one in spirit. Jonathan loved David as himself.
	David later took care of Jonathan's son, Mephibosheth, who couldn't walk.
	Jonathan told Saul that David was innocent.
	Jonathan warned David that Saul was trying to kill him.
	Jonathan promised to let David know if Saul intended to harm him. He asked David to show kindness to him and his family.

20-C David Respects God's Anointed

Because Saul was trying to kill him, David ran for his life. David had a number of men loyal to him, and they all hid in the wilderness. This time was very difficult for David. He could not go home or be with his family. David had been anointed years ago, but he was still waiting for God to make him king.

► Read **1 Samuel 26:7–25** and complete the following sentences.

⊙ **Verse 7** – _____ and _____ sneak into Saul's camp at night.

⊙ **Verse 8** – Abishai wants to _____ Saul with a spear into the ground.

- **Verse 9-10** – David asks who could hurt the Lord's _____ and be guiltless. David says that God might one day end Saul's life, or the king might go into battle and die.

- **Verse 11-12** – For now, David takes Saul's _____ and a _____ of water, escaping the camp without being caught.

- **Verse 18** – David asks Saul why the king is pursuing his own _____. What evil did David do to deserve this?

- **Verse 21** – Saul admits his sin and promises not to _____ David. Saul blesses David, and the two go their separate ways.

The Death of Saul

Some time later, the Philistines attacked Israel again. This time, the battle did not go well for Saul's army. The Philistines killed three of Saul's sons—including Jonathan, who fought alongside his father to the end. As the enemy closed in on Saul, the king fell on his own sword and died.

Afterward, an Amalekite brought David the news that the king was dead. The Amalekite even claimed that he had killed Saul himself. As proof, he showed Saul's crown and armband.

▶ Read **2 Samuel 1:1-10**. Why do you think the Amalekite told David that he had killed Saul?

_____

_____

_____

_____

▶ Continue reading **2 Samuel 1:11-16** and mark how David showed his feelings about the deaths of Saul and Jonathan. Mark all that apply.

☐ Shouted for joy	☐ Tore his clothes	☐ Mourned and fasted
☐ Hunted the Philistines who killed the king's three sons	☐ Praised the Amalekite for doing his duty to Israel	☐ Had the Amalekite executed for claiming to kill God's anointed
☐ Proclaimed a day of celebration	☐ Blamed God for the death of Saul	☐ Wished that he had never been anointed

Possessing the Land

▶ Think of what you've learned about Saul and David so far. Complete the chart below by explaining how Saul and David were different from each other.

	Saul	David
How did they respond to God's commands?		
How did they help their nation?		
Who did they choose to serve?		

Remember, both David and Saul stood out. They were both good-looking, strong, and respected. But none of that was as important as their attitudes toward God.

LESSON 21
The Reign of David

Vocabulary

- **Census** – A count of all people in a group or nation

- **Seer** – An older word for *prophet*; used in the time of David

- **Blot Out** – To wipe away or erase

- **Iniquity** – A wicked or evil action; a sin

21-A The Second King

Soon after the death of Saul, David became king. But his difficulties were not over. Saul's old followers fought against David, and enemy nations continued to attack Israel. David the king needed God just as much as David the shepherd had needed Him.

▶ How did David respond to his problems? Read the following passages and fill in the blanks.

Passage	David's Problem	David's Response
2 Samuel 5:17–19	The _____ began to hunt for him. (v. 17)	He asked the _____ if he should fight them. (v. 19)
1 Chronicles 13:2–11	He wanted the _____ brought to Jerusalem. (v. 3)	He put it on a _____ instead of having priests carry it the way that God commanded. (v. 7)
1 Chronicles 15:1–2	He prepared a place for the ark in Jerusalem.	He had the _____ carry the ark this time.
1 Chronicles 22:6–8, 14–17	He wanted a _____ for God (v. 7), but God said that he should not be the one to build it.	He gave _____ his son everything needed to build the Temple. (v. 17)

Just as He had with Abraham, Isaac, and Jacob, God made several promises to David. Some of these promises were for Israel, and some were for David's own descendants.

▶ God gave promises to David through the prophet Nathan. Read **2 Samuel 7:8–16** and match each verse below to its promise.

Verse 9	Verse 10	Verse 11	Verse 12	Verse 14

	God will give His people their own place, where their enemies will no longer bother them.
	God will establish a kingdom from David's descendants.
	God will act like a father to David's son.
	God will make David's name great.
	God will give David rest from his enemies.

21-B David Counts His Men

God called David "a man after His own heart," but that doesn't mean David was perfect. Sometimes he chose to ignore God's commands and do things his own way. Sometimes he trusted his own wisdom and strength instead of the Lord's.

One time during David's rule, he was tempted to take a **census** of all the men in Israel who could fight as soldiers. There was nothing wrong with counting people, but David's motive was probably sinful. Maybe he trusted his army more than he trusted God. Maybe he wanted more authority than what God allowed. We're not sure why the census was sinful, but Scripture shows us that it was.

▶ Read **1 Chronicles 21:1–28** and answer the following questions.

⊙ When David commands Joab and the other leaders to take the census, does Joab think it is a good idea? (vv. 3–4) ☐ Yes ☐ No

⊙ How does Joab keep David from knowing the full number of men? (vv. 5–6)

_____

_____

⊙ After God punishes the kingdom, how does David describe what he did? (vv. 7–8)

_____

_____

⊙ Does King David's sin affect him alone? (vv. 7–13) ☐ Yes ☐ No

⊙ What are the results of David's sin? (vv. 14–15)

_____

_____

_____

⊙ In this passage, did David take responsibility for his actions? How do you know?

_____

_____

_____

_____

⊙ Why did David insist on buying the Jebusite's threshing floor at full price? (vv. 22–26)

_____

_____

_____

_____

David was not perfect. Like all of us, he sinned against God. But when he realized that he had sinned, he confessed it to God and accepted the consequences. His heart ached until it was right with God.

21-C David Repents

► Read all of **Psalm 51**, which David wrote after he realized that he had sinned against God. Once you've read the psalm, read the following statements and mark them as true or false. Write the verses that helped you decide.

Statement	True or False?		Verses
David thought that God owed him forgiveness.	☐ True	☐ False	
David said that he had sinned against God, and only God.	☐ True	☐ False	
David begged God to **blot out** all his **iniquities**.	☐ True	☐ False	
David wanted God to create a pure or clean heart in him.	☐ True	☐ False	
God desires burnt offerings more than any other kind.	☐ True	☐ False	

► How would you describe David's attitude in this psalm?

_____

_____

_____

_____

► Look at **verses 13–19** again. Do you think David believed that God would forgive him? Explain your answer.

_____

_____

_____

_____

Possessing the Land

► How do you respond when you fail or do something wrong? For each sentence below, mark what you tend to do most often.

When my parents or guardians catch me disobeying them, I . . .

☐ deny that I did anything wrong.	☐ admit that I did something wrong.	☐ blame someone or something else.

When I realize that I was wrong about something, I . . .

☐ insist that what I said wasn't wrong.	☐ admit I was wrong and try to learn for next time.	☐ hope no one remembers what I said.

When something bad happens because of what I chose to do, I . . .

☐ pretend I had nothing to do with it.	☐ try to take responsibility for what I did.	☐ blame someone or something else.

When I don't get what I want, I . . .

☐ get angry at others.	☐ keep begging.	☐ complain.
☐ pretend I never wanted it in the first place.	☐ accept it and trust God to do what's best for me.	☐ give up ever trying to get what I want.

LESSON 22
The Reign of Solomon

Vocabulary

- **Wisdom** – The ability to use knowledge well; insight and understanding

- **Discern** – To see the differences between one thing and another; to know good from evil

- **Proverb** – A wise saying; a short statement that teaches a general principle

- **Alliance** – An agreement between nations; a promise not to attack, but to cooperate

22-A The Third King

David was a better king than Saul had been. David sometimes did wrong, but he also repented quickly after his sin. He followed God his entire life, trusting the Lord to lead him through difficult times. Now he faced one more test.

▶ Read the following verses from the beginning of **1 Kings 2** and answer the questions.

- ◉ **Verse 1** – When King David nears his death, who does he speak with?

  _____

- ◉ **Verses 2–3** – In your own words, what does the king tell this person to do?

  _____

  _____

  _____

  _____

  _____

⊙ **Verse 4** – If David's descendants do these things, what does God promise in return?

_____

_____

Not only did David want to remain in close fellowship with God, but he also wanted his son to do the same.

▶ What made Solomon such a special king? Read **1 Kings 3:1–15** and fill in the chart below.

Verses 3–4	If Solomon loved the Lord and worshiped the best he could, write a **W**. If he rejected his father and his God, write an **I**.	
Verse 7	If Solomon compared himself to a child, write an **I**. If he compared himself to a mighty warrior, write a **D**.	
Verse 9	If Solomon asked God for wealth and power, write an **I**. If he asked for a discerning or understanding heart, write an **S**.	
Verse 10	If God was displeased with Solomon's request, write an **O**. If God was pleased with Solomon's request, write a **D**.	
Verses 11–13	If Solomon received only what he asked for, write a **C**. If he received riches and honor as well, write an **O**.	
Verse 14	If God promised Solomon a long life for his obedience, write an **M**. If God promised Solomon a large army for his obedience, write a **Y**.	

Note the word spelled out in the chart above. This is what God gave Solomon. God showed the king how to understand and lead wisely. Solomon learned how to **discern** between right and wrong.

▶ Read **1 Kings 3:28**. What does God's wisdom help Solomon do?

_____

▶ Read **Proverbs 16:16** to see how much Solomon valued wisdom. Fill in the summaries below:

⊙ It's much better to get _____ than it is to get _____.

⊙ It's better to choose _____ than _____.

God was more generous than Solomon could have ever imagined. The king received as much wisdom as he wanted, and he recorded much of it in the Book of **Proverbs**. This collection of sayings, which we'll study in Lesson 29, can help people live wisely.

22-B Building the Temple

God did not allow David to build the Temple, but the time had come for Solomon to complete this task. Solomon had all the supplies that his father had gathered for him. He hired the most skilled workers to build it. He wanted the finished building to be a beautiful reminder of God's power, holiness, and love.

► Read the following verses and fill in the blanks.

1 Kings 5:4	God gave Solomon _____ on every side. While the Temple was being built, he didn't have to defend against enemies or other troubles.
1 Kings 5:8–10	King Hiram gave timber cut from cedar and _____ trees.
1 Kings 6:1	Construction began in the _____th year after Israel left Egypt.
1 Kings 6:37–38	• The foundation was completed in the _____ year of Solomon's reign. • The entire Temple was finished in the _____ year. • That means it took _____ years to build the Temple.
1 Kings 8:21	In the Temple, Solomon made a place for the _____, which held the covenant of the Lord.

The Temple became a beautiful monument to God. The building materials were massive, with one stone measuring over 38 feet long. Gold covered much of the structure. Nothing else compared to it.

When construction was finished, all of Israel came to Jerusalem to dedicate the Temple to God. The priests carried in all the special furniture and vessels, including the Ark of the Covenant. Everyone offered sacrifices to the Lord, and Solomon himself knelt before the altar to praise God. The Lord had blessed His people, and they celebrated together for 14 days.

▶ Read **1 Kings 7:48–50** and draw at least four of these furnishings in the space below.

22-C God's Covenant with Solomon

▶ After Solomon finished building the Temple, God appeared to him in another dream. Read about this in **1 Kings 9:1–7** and answer the following questions.

⊙ What does God promise to do if Solomon obeys like his father David? (vv. 4–5)

_____

_____

⊙ What will happen if Solomon or his sons serve and worship other gods? (vv. 6–8)

_____

_____

God valued faithfulness more than anything that Solomon could build or offer to Him. He wanted the king to worship Him and Him alone. As long as Solomon followed God, he found wisdom and peace.

▶ Solomon did not keep his gifts to himself. He made **alliances** with other nations and traded with them. Read **1 Kings 10:1–13** and mark each statement as true or false.

The Queen of Sheba traveled to Jerusalem by herself, secretly.	☐ True	☐ False
Solomon answered all the queen's questions.	☐ True	☐ False
The queen was not impressed by Solomon's wisdom or wealth.	☐ True	☐ False
The queen praised God for setting Solomon on the throne of Israel.	☐ True	☐ False
Solomon and the queen gave each other enormous gifts.	☐ True	☐ False

► Sadly, Solomon did not always treasure God or His wisdom. As he grew older, he turned further and further away from God. Read **1 Kings 11:1–11** and answer the following.

  ⊙ What kind of sins does Solomon commit? (vv. 1–8)

_____

_____

_____

  ⊙ What does God tell Solomon will happen? (v. 11)

_____

_____

Solomon ruled over Israel at the height of its wealth, power, and influence. But after the king's death, the kingdom broke apart, and peace ended.

Possessing the Land

Those who follow Jesus do not need a temple like the one Solomon built. If you've accepted Christ's gift of salvation, God lives inside of you. You can worship God anywhere and anytime. He cares much more about your heart than He cares about fancy buildings or rituals.

► Read **1 Corinthians 6:19–20**. We should take care of our bodies just as we might care for a temple. If the Holy Spirit lives in us, we honor or dishonor God by what we say and do. In the spaces below, describe briefly how you can build a "temple" to God in each area.

  ⊙ My attitudes: _____

_____

_____

_____

  ⊙ My relationships with others: _____

_____

_____

_____

  ⊙ My responsibilities: _____

_____

_____

_____

LESSON 23
Elijah and Elisha

Vocabulary

- **Revolt** – To rebel against a ruler or some other authority; to break or turn away

- **Ba'al** – An Old Testament name for many kinds of false gods; can mean "lord" or "ruler"

- **Successor** – Someone who takes the place and responsibilities of another

23-A The Divided Kingdom

When a king of Israel chose to sin, the entire nation faced the consequences. As Solomon neared the end of his life, more and more problems threatened Israel.

► Solomon had a few enemies among other nations, but one problem came from within Israel itself. Read **1 Kings 11:26–33** and fill in the blanks below.

Verse 28	_____ was a brave man with a good reputation. He worked hard, so Solomon put him in charge of the workers from the tribe of Joseph.
Verses 29–30	While he was traveling, Jeroboam met the prophet named _____. The prophet tore his new robe into twelve pieces to represent the twelve tribes.
Verse 31	The prophet told Jeroboam to take _____ pieces for himself. God would give Jeroboam this many tribes to rule.
Verse 32	But David's descendants would have _____ tribe, as God promised.
Verse 33	God was tearing the kingdom away because the people _____ false gods like Ashtoreth and Chemosh.

God said that He would preserve Jeroboam's line so long as the man obeyed God's law like David did. But Solomon tried to kill this would-be king, so Jeroboam fled to Egypt and lived there until after Solomon died.

▶ Read the following verses from **1 Kings 12** and mark the correct answers.

⦿ **Verse 4** – What do the people ask the new king Rehoboam to do?

☐ **Lighten their work**   ☐ **Give them time off**   ☐ **Make their work more difficult**

⦿ **Verses 6–7** – What do the older advisors say that Rehoboam should do?

☐ **Give up the throne**   ☐ **Punish the people**   ☐ **Give the people what they asked**

⦿ **Verse 8–11** – What do Rehoboam's younger friends tell him to do?

☐ **Make the people work harder**   ☐ **Help the people**   ☐ **Run away**

⦿ **Verses 12–15** – Whose advice does Rehoboam take?

☐ **The elders**   ☐ **His friends**

⦿ **Verses 16–19** – How do the people respond to the king's decision?

☐ **Most of Israel *revolt* against him.**   ☐ **They laugh.**   ☐ **They work harder.**

▶ So Jeroboam became king over the ten tribes that rejected Rehoboam. Rehoboam wanted to take back what he lost, but God told him to stop. Read **1 Kings 12:22–24** and explain why God told all the soldiers to go home.

_____

_____

Even though the kingdom split over human choices and human failures, God allowed it to happen. He fulfilled His promises to Solomon and to Jeroboam. This was God's judgment on the people for turning toward false gods. The people had rebelled against God before they ever rebelled against a king.

There were now two separate kingdoms:

The Kingdom of Israel	The Kingdom of Judah
Began with **King Jeroboam,** the son of Nebat	Began with **King Rehoboam,** the son of Solomon
Was in the **North**	Was in the **South**
Lasted **209 years**	Lasted **345 years**
Fell to the **Assyrians**	Fell to the **Babylonians**
Had **20 kings**, all of them ungodly	Had **19 kings and 1 queen**, with some good and some bad

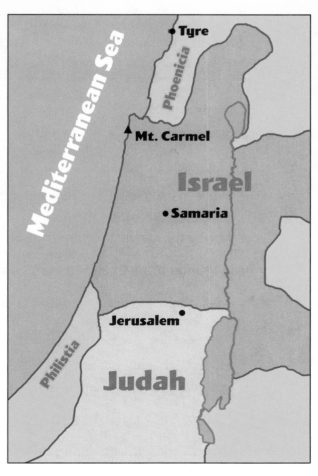

23-B Elijah the Prophet

Things got worse and worse for Israel. The people continued to worship false gods, copying the terrible sins of other nations. The Israelites no longer seemed like a people chosen by God. During the 300–400 years after Solomon, very few Israelite rulers followed God.

But God did not need kings or queens to help His people. He sent other kinds of leaders to draw Israel back to Himself. Prophets arose to share God's message. One of these prophets was a man named Elijah. He lived in the northern kingdom of Israel, which was ruled by King Ahab and Queen Jezebel.

► How does **1 Kings 16:33** describe Ahab?

_____

_____

► Note what **1 Kings 18:4** and **13** say about Jezebel. What was she doing to God's prophets?

_____

While many other prophets needed to hide, God showed His power through Elijah. The Lord used this prophet to perform many miracles to prove that He was the one true God. Maybe the greatest of these miracles took place on Mount Carmel.

► Read **1 Kings 18:16–21** and answer the following questions.

⊙ After Ahab calls Elijah a troublemaker, what does the prophet say that the king did? (v. 18)

_____

_____

⊙ Who will Ahab bring with him to Mt. Carmel? (v. 19)

_____

_____

► This would be a showdown unlike any other. Continue reading in **1 Kings 18:22–29**.

⊙ According to Elijah, what will the true God do to the sacrifices? (v. 24)

_____

⊙ Do the prophets of Ba'al have any success? (vv. 25–29) ☐ Yes ☐ No

To remove all doubt of God's power, Elijah asked people to soak his altar and sacrifice with water. He even dug a trench, which filled with water too. Elijah then prayed to God to accept his sacrifice.

► Finally, read **1 Kings 18:36–39**.

⊙ What happens to Elijah's sacrifice? (v. 38)

_____

_____

_____

⊙ How do the people respond? (v. 39)

_____

_____

23-C Elijah's Successor, Elisha

Though God showed His power on Mount Carmel, most of the Israelites went back to worshiping Ba'al. They knew Ba'al wasn't real, but they hated God so much that they would rather worship a lifeless idol than Him. Elijah became very discouraged, but God gave the prophet some hope for the future.

► Read what God said in **1 Kings 19:15–18** and answer the following questions.

⊙ Besides anointing two new kings, who does Elijah anoint to replace him? (v. 16)

_____

⊙ At this time, how many people still follow God in Israel? (v. 18) _____

► When Elijah's ministry was over, God chose to take him away. Read how in **2 Kings 2:7–14**.

⊙ What does Elisha ask Elijah to give him? (v. 9)

_____

⊙ What happens to Elijah? (v. 11)

_____

_____

◉ Does Elisha get what he asked for? How do you know? (vv. 13–14)

_____

_____

As He did with Elijah, God worked many great miracles through Elisha. During times of famine, Elisha provided food and water for the needy, and he also healed the sick. God showed His power to anyone who cared to look. Unfortunately, most Israelites still rejected God and His Law.

► Read each situation below and match it to the miracle that God performed.

	2 Kings 2:19–22	A city's water supply was corrupted.		**A.** Elisha promised that God would give her what she wanted in a year.
	2 Kings 2:23–24	Some young men blocked Elisha from going to Bethel.		**B.** God sent two bears to attack them.
	2 Kings 4:1–7	A widow needed money to pay back a debt.		**C.** Elisha threw salt, and God removed the problem.
	2 Kings 4:8, 14–16	A kind woman hoped for a son.		**D.** After he washed in the Jordan River seven times, God healed him.
	2 Kings 4:18–20, 35–37	The kind woman's son died.		**E.** God made oil pour continually from a single jar.
	2 Kings 5:1–3, 9–14	Naaman, a Syrian military leader, had leprosy.		**F.** God brought him back.

Possessing the Land

Many rulers of Israel and Judah did not follow God. Instead, they led people deep into sin.

▶ What can happen if a government official doesn't tell the truth?

_____

_____

_____

▶ What can happen if a pastor or church leader doesn't know God's Word?

_____

_____

_____

Even if we have bad rulers, we can still lead people closer to God. Every one of us can be a leader—no matter our age or ability. We may not be a king or queen, but we can always do the right thing and encourage others to do the same.

▶ Who notices your behavior? Who watches what you do or listens to what you say?

_____

_____

▶ Even if things are difficult, how can you be a better leader for these people?

_____

_____

_____

_____

Ezra the Teacher

Vocabulary

- **Exile** – To drive out someone from their home country; to banish or separate

- **Babylonian Exile** – The time when many Jews were forced to live in Babylon (600s–500s BC)

- **Providence** – God's work through human or natural events

- **Magistrate** – A government official that helps apply and enforce the law

24-A Rebuilding God's Temple

Much of Israel continued to disobey God and worship idols, so God allowed them to suffer under invading armies.

- The northern kingdom of Israel was taken over by the Assyrian army. The Assyrians **exiled** the Israelites and brought other people to live in the land. The kingdom was no more.

- In the south, the Babylonians conquered the kingdom of Judah. They destroyed much of Jerusalem, including Solomon's Temple. They left the land in ruin. Even worse, they captured many Jews and brought them to serve in the city of Babylon. This began the **Babylonian Exile**.

But God would never abandon His people. He sent prophets to explain that after 70 years, Israel would be able to return home. Sure enough, when Babylon was conquered by the Persians, the new king Cyrus declared that all captive nations could return home. The Jews could now go back and rebuild their country.

The story of Ezra begins during this time. This book explains how God gave the Jews what they needed to rebuild. Through His **providence**, God protected and helped the people. They could rebuild their homes, their cities, and even the Temple. They could worship God like their ancestors once did.

► How did the people rebuild the Temple? Read the following verses from **Ezra 3** and mark the correct ending to each statement.

Verse 2: Before anything else, they build . . .

☐ a giant statue to honor King Cyrus.	☐ the walls of the Temple.	☐ an altar to make burnt offerings to God.

Verse 7: Just like Solomon did for his Temple, they buy . . .

☐ special golden robes for each priest.	☐ cedar trees from Lebanon.	☐ all the silver that the people can afford.

Verses 10–11: When the foundation of the Temple is complete, the priests . . .

☐ stopped all building for ten years.	☐ dig it up and start over on a second one.	☐ sing praises to God.

Verse 12: Some older people who remember Solomon's Temple . . .

☐ weep because the new Temple isn't as good.	☐ help carry stone bricks.	☐ pray next to the new foundation.

► Continue reading the following verses from **Ezra 4** and mark the correct ending to each sentence.

Verses 4–5: The enemies of the Jews try to stop the building by . . .

☐ paying people in Cyrus' government to oppose the Jews.	☐ stealing over a hundred cedar trees.	☐ threatening to set the city of Jerusalem on fire.

Verses 12–13: These enemies tell Cyrus that if he lets Jerusalem be rebuilt . . .

☐ the city could become the king's new capital.	☐ the Jews will no longer pay taxes or tribute.	☐ the Jews will be very grateful.

Verses 21–22: After hearing from the enemies of the Jews, Cyrus decides to . . .

☐ ignore them and let Jerusalem be rebuilt.	☐ send armies to destroy everyone in Israel.	☐ order all rebuilding stopped in Jerusalem.

The enemies of the Jews seemed to be winning. As a result, very little happened in Jerusalem until Cyrus died.

The next king was named Darius. The Jews sent him a letter asking for permission to continue their work.

▶ Read **Ezra 6:7–10**. How does King Darius respond to the Jews' request?

_____

_____

_____

_____

▶ Continue reading **Ezra 6:14–18** and answer the following questions.

⊙ When is the new Temple finished? (v. 15)

_____

⊙ What do the people do when the Temple is dedicated to God? (v. 16)

_____

24-B Ezra Comes to Jerusalem

God sent several leaders to help the people as they returned to Jerusalem. One of these leaders was a teacher named Ezra.

▶ Read the following verses from **Ezra 7** and fill in the blanks.

Verse 6	Ezra was a _____ who knew the Law of Moses. God's hand was with him, so he had favor with King Artaxerxes.
Verses 7–9	Ezra led some Israelites from Babylon back to _____.
Verse 10	Ezra wanted to teach the Law of the Lord in _____.

Verses 11–13	King _____ sent a letter with Ezra. This letter decreed that any Israelite could go back to Jerusalem with Ezra.
Verses 14–16	Ezra brought the Law, along with a lot of _____ and _____. The people could buy whatever they needed for the Temple in Jerusalem.
Verse 25	The king encouraged Ezra to appoint _____ and judges in Israel. These would carry out the Law that Ezra taught the people.

▶ Why do you think the people needed to be taught God's Law?

_____

_____

24-C Returning to God's Law

During the exile, many Jews spent years without worshiping God or following His Law. Many built their lives around false gods and sin. They continued doing the things that brought God's judgment in the first place. But now that Israel had rebuilt the Temple and heard God's Law again, they knew what God expected them to do.

▶ Read **Ezra 9:1–12** and answer the following questions.

⊙ What problem do the leaders tell Ezra about? (vv. 1–2)

_____

_____

⊙ Why is this a problem? (vv. 10–12)

_____

_____

_____

⊙ What three words would you use to describe how Ezra feels about the people's sin? (vv. 6–7)

_____

▶ Think back to what you learned about King Solomon. When he married many different wives who didn't worship God, what sin did he practice? Look at **1 Kings 11:1–6** if you don't remember.

_____

There was nothing wrong with marrying people from other nations. Remember that Rahab, Ruth, and many others joined God's people with His blessing. But God did not want His children to marry those who worshiped false gods. He did not want anything to tempt His people to turn away from Him and be hurt by sin.

▶ Read **Ezra 10:1**. How do the people feel when they realize what they did?

_____

_____

▶ Finally, read **Ezra 10:2–4**. What do the leaders of Israel choose to do about the problem?

_____

_____

This was very difficult, but the people did not see any other option. Ezra chose people to judge all of the marriage cases. For each case, the judges decided what God's Law allowed and what was best to do. The people took their sin seriously and tried to find a way to please God.

Possessing the Land

Like any good leader, Ezra depended on God. He humbly followed God and taught others how to obey His commands.

▶ Read each summary below and write the character traits that you believe Ezra showed. You can write traits more than once.

| Faith in God | Devotion to God | Humility | Courage | Patience | Gratitude |

Passage	Summary	Traits
Ezra 1–6	In his book, Ezra wrote all about how God helped the people rebuild the Temple. He carefully recorded what happened and who was involved.	
Ezra 7:9; 8:31–32	Ezra led the Jews back to Jerusalem. They traveled for four months, sometimes through dangerous territory.	
Ezra 7:10	Ezra dedicated himself to studying and teaching the Law of the Lord.	
Ezra 7:27–28	Ezra blessed God for helping Israel through King Artaxerxes.	

Passage	Summary	Traits
Ezra 8:21–23	Ezra asked God to protect the Jews as they traveled back to Jerusalem.	
Ezra 9:3–5	Ezra was heartbroken over the people's sin. He begged God to forgive them.	

▶ Choose one of the character traits you just listed. Write a prayer asking God to help you better show this trait.

_____

_____

_____

_____

_____

_____

Vocabulary

• **Leadership** – The ability to lead others; for believers, helping people follow God

The Temple in Jerusalem was rebuilt, but it did not have the same beauty or magnificence as Solomon's Temple did. Around the Temple, the city looked even worse. The walls had fallen, the gates had burned, and many buildings lay in ruin.

But God had not forgotten His people. He prepared someone to help the people returning from exile. Thirteen years after the building of the Temple, a Jewish man living in Persia heard about the troubles in Jerusalem.

25-A Nehemiah's Mission

► Read **Nehemiah 2:1–10** and number the events below in order from **1** to **8**.

	When Nehemiah travels back toward Judah, the king sends soldiers and horsemen with him.
	King Artaxerxes asks Nehemiah why he looks so sad.
	The king asks what Nehemiah wants from him.
	Nehemiah asks the king to send him to Judah so he can rebuild Jerusalem.
	Nehemiah hears that Jerusalem is in ruins and begins to pray.
	Two men named Sanballat and Tobiah are unhappy that anyone is trying to help the people of Israel.
	Nehemiah also asks the king for letters that will give permission and help for the rebuilding in Jerusalem.
	Nehemiah tells the king that Jerusalem is a broken, burned ruin.

▶ Continue reading **Nehemiah 2:11–20** and answer the following questions.

◉ What does Nehemiah do first when he arrives in Jerusalem? (vv. 12–15)

_____

_____

In a time when so many people hated the Jews, a wall could help the city stay safe. Without a wall, Jerusalem had little defense against its enemies.

◉ Does Nehemiah ask others to help fix this problem? (vv. 16–18)
☐ Yes ☐ No

◉ What do Sanballat and Tobiah do when the Jews start rebuilding the wall? (vv. 19–20)

_____

_____

_____

_____

_____

◉ How does Nehemiah respond to these two men? (v. 20)

_____

_____

_____

25-B Facing Opposition

▶ The people in Jerusalem faced many problems as they tried to rebuild the city. Read the following passages and fill in the blanks.

Passage	The Problem	The Response
Nehemiah 4:1–6	Sanballat and Tobiah mocked the Jews, saying that a _____ walking on the wall would break it down. (v. 3)	Nehemiah prayed that God would judge them for their mockery. The people kept working on the wall until it was _____ done. (v. 6)

Passage	The Problem	The Response
Nehemiah 4:7–9	The enemies of Israel planned to fight against _____. (v. 8)	The Jews prayed to God and set a _____ to look out for danger during the day and night. (v. 9)
Nehemiah 4:10–14	The strength of the people was _____. There was also far too much _____ in the way of the wall. (v. 10)	Nehemiah posted guards at the lower gaps in the wall. He told the people not to be afraid but instead remember the _____. (v. 14)

Sanballat and Tobiah continued to oppose Nehemiah and the others rebuilding the city. There were plots to murder Nehemiah, and even some of his own people spied on him. Despite all this, God continued to bless the work.

▶ Read **Nehemiah 6:15–16** and answer the following questions.

⊙ Does God help the people finish the wall?　　☐ Yes　☐ No

⊙ How long do the Jews work on the wall? _____

⊙ How do the Jews' enemies react to the news?

_____

_____

25-C Lessons on Leadership

Nehemiah was a good leader because he loved God and other people. The man led well by following God and helping others do the same. And if we want to become better leaders, we can study the perfect example of **leadership** in Jesus Christ.

▶ Read **Matthew 20:20–28** and mark the correct answers to the following questions.

⊙ **Verse 20** – Who has a request for Jesus?
☐ **Zebedee**　　☐ **the mother of Zebedee's sons (James and John)**　　☐ **an angel**

⊙ **Verse 21** – What is the request?
☐ **twenty pieces of silver**　　☐ **places of honor for her sons**　　☐ **healing for Zebedee**

⊙ **Verse 24** – How do the other ten disciples feel about this request?

☐ **supportive**   ☐ **sad**   ☐ **indignant, angry**

⊙ **Verses 25–27** – What does Jesus say is the way to greatness?

☐ **strength, authority**   ☐ **speaking well**   ☐ **service, ministry**

⊙ **Verse 28** – Who does Jesus offer as an example of leadership?

☐ **David the king**   ☐ **the Son of Man**   ☐ **Deborah the judge**

⊙ **Verse 28** – How does this person show greatness and leadership?

☐ **by serving and dying for others**   ☐ **by having many followers**   ☐ **good looks**

▶ Read **John 13:12–17** and answer the following questions.

⊙ What has Jesus just finished doing for the disciples? (v. 12)

_____

_____

⊙ Why should Jesus' followers do the same thing? (vv. 14–17)

_____

_____

_____

▶ In your reading, what lessons did Jesus teach His followers? Check all you think apply.

☐	We should wash our friends' feet every day.
☐	We should be willing to serve others.
☐	We should never get our feet dirty.
☐	We should dress in the same clothes that Jesus did.
☐	A godly leader serves others like Jesus did.
☐	We should humble ourselves enough to do what God wants.
☐	It's wrong to get help from other people.
☐	We can't take true greatness for ourselves. God gives it to those who serve.
☐	Every believer serves others the same way.
☐	Only weak people should be humble.
☐	The nicest thing you can do for people is to wash their feet.
☐	We can find blessing by helping others.

Possessing the Land

Sometimes you will be mocked for doing a good thing. What do you think you should do in that situation?

▶ Read the story below and then write an ending that shows how Sophia could respond while reflecting Jesus.

Sophia walked briskly down the sidewalk in her town. Behind her, she pulled a cart filled with brown grocery bags. Some of these held canned food and boxes, while others were empty. She stopped at the next house and knocked on the door. A lady answered, somewhat nervous to see a young person on her porch.

"Hi!" Sophia said warmly. "My church is collecting food for people hurt by the big storm last month. I'm gathering some cans and dry goods. Would you like to contribute anything?"

The lady smiled, asked Sophia to wait a moment, and came back to the door with two bags of food.

Sophia felt great as she headed to the next house. She enjoyed seeing people help out, and it was awesome to show others God's care. She almost didn't notice the two boys across the road laughing at her. She didn't feel safe, so she kept walking as they called out.

"Hey—hey you! What're you doing? What's that there?"

Sophia decided to stop. Without looking up, she said, "I'm collecting food for the flood victims. Would you like to—"

"Oh, sure," one of the boys laughed. "Like you and your little wagon can do anything. Quit showing off. What are these? Beans? Who likes beans?"

Before she could do anything, they kicked over her cart and ran away, laughing. Food spilled onto the road. She felt like crying.

▶ _____

_____

_____

_____

_____

_____

_____

_____

Queen Esther

Vocabulary

- **Banquet / Feast** – An elegant meal, often for a large group of people

- **Decree** – A law given by a ruler like a king or queen; a public command

- **Fasting** – Choosing not to eat, often to focus on praying or some other spiritual activity

- **Chronicles / Annals** – A historical record; a book about the events in a nation or kingdom

26-A Esther Becomes Queen

Even though the Jews could now go back to their homeland, not all of them did so. During the years of exile, many began new lives with new families and new homes. Children were born who had no memory of Israel. Many Jews simply stayed where they were.

Esther and Mordecai were two such Jews who did not return to Israel. They instead lived in the Persian city of Susa. Even though they weren't in the promised land, God still worked through them to keep His covenant with Israel. While many Jews thought God had forgotten them, He would prove them wrong.

▶ The first two chapters of Esther show how God placed Esther and Mordecai where they could help their people. Read the following passages and fill in the blanks.

Esther 1:1–3	The king of Persia gave a huge _____ for all his nobles and important government officials.
Esther 1:10–11	While celebrating, the king told his servants to bring Queen _____ so he could show her off like a trophy.
Esther 1:12	She _____ to obey the king's command, so the king became _____.

Esther 1:19–21	The nobles worried that this would lead all women to disrespect their husbands. One said that the king should make a **decree** that _____ could no longer appear before the king. The noble also said that the king should give her royal _____ to someone else. The king decided to follow the noble's advice.
Esther 2:5–8	Esther was a Jewish girl living in Susa. After her parents died, she was adopted and raised by her cousin, _____. When the king began searching for a new queen, Esther and many other women were taken to him.
Esther 2:16–20	The king chose _____ over the other women, so he made her the new queen. He threw a great feast in her honor, but she did not tell anyone that she was Jewish.

► How do you think Esther felt in this situation? Why?

_____

_____

_____

_____

_____

► God was also preparing Mordecai to help the Jews. Continue reading in **Esther 2:19–23** and answer the questions below.

⊙ Where does Mordecai sit? (v. 19) _____

⊙ Here he can see much of what happens at the palace. What does Mordecai hear two men planning to do? (vv. 21–22)

_____

_____

⊙ What does Mordecai do about this? (v. 22)

_____

⊙ Does the evil plan succeed? (v. 23) ☐ Yes ☐ No

⊙ Where is this event recorded? (v. 23)

_____

_____

26-B Haman's Plot

▶ Read **Esther 3:1–13** and then number the events in order from **1** to **7**.

	The king promotes Haman the Agagite to a place higher than the other nobles.
	The king and Haman drink together while the people of Susa wonder what happened.
	Haman becomes extremely angry with Mordecai.
	Knowing that Mordecai is a Jew, Haman tells the king that a certain group of people should be destroyed.
	People ask Mordecai why he disobeyed the king and refused to bow.
	Almost everyone bows down to Haman—but not Mordecai.
	The king signs a decree that all the Jews should be killed later that year.

▶ Read the following verses from **Esther 4** and mark the correct ending to each sentence.

Verse 1: When Mordecai hears about the king's decree, he feels . . .

☐ afraid and sorrowful.   ☐ happy and excited.   ☐ annoyed.

Verses 6–9: Mordecai sends a message telling Esther to . . .

☐ run away from the palace to live in Israel.   ☐ kill Haman.   ☐ plead with the king on behalf of the Jews.

Verses 10–11: Mordecai's plan is dangerous because . . .

☐ the king might execute Mordecai for talking to the queen.   ☐ if the king doesn't hold out his scepter to Esther when she goes to his court, she could die.   ☐ the king does not like to be bothered about the problems of the Jews.

Verses 12–14: Even if Esther stays silent, she is in danger because . . .

☐ she is Jewish.   ☐ the king wants a new queen.   ☐ the kingdom will soon come under attack.

Verses 15–16: Esther agrees to Mordecai's request, and she asks him to . . .

☐ go with her to talk to the king.   ☐ throw a banquet for Haman.   ☐ gather the Jews for a time of **fasting**.

▶ Note **Esther 4:14** again. Do you think Mordecai believed that God would protect Israel no matter what?

☐ Yes   ☐ No

▶ When Esther appeared in the royal court, who do you think had more power on their side—the king or the queen? Explain your answer.

_____

_____

_____

_____

▶ Read what happened in **Esther 5:1–4**. What does Esther ask the king?

_____

_____

26-C God Saves His People

A banquet with your greatest enemy? Esther's request was surprising, but this would give her the chance to talk with the king about Haman and the Jews.

▶ At the first banquet, Esther said nothing about her problem. In **Esther 5:6–8**, what does the queen ask for, instead?

_____

_____

▶ Read **Esther 5:9–14** and answer the following questions.

  ⊙ Despite everything good Haman has, why does it all seem worthless to him? (vv. 9, 13)

_____

_____

⊙ What does Haman's wife Zeresh tell him to do? (v. 14)

_____

_____

⊙ Does Haman follow his wife's advice? ☐ Yes ☐ No

That same night, the king couldn't sleep, so he told his servants to read aloud through the royal chronicles. When he heard the part about Mordecai saving his life, the king asked how Mordecai had been rewarded. But no reward had ever been given.

▶ Just then, Haman entered the outer court of the palace. Read **Esther 6:4** and think about what Haman wanted to ask the king. In this moment, which words would you use to describe Haman? Check all you think apply.

☐ proud	☐ forgiving	☐ envious	☐ merciful	☐ humble
☐ honorable	☐ grateful	☐ wicked	☐ patient	☐ confident

▶ Continue reading **Esther 6:6–12**. Explain in your own words why Haman is surprised.

_____

_____

_____

_____

_____

Haman hated Mordecai all the more. He was filled with rage, but it was time to go to Esther's second banquet.

▶ Read **Esther 7:3–6**. What does Esther ask the king this time?

_____

_____

Esther explained that Haman planned to kill her people, the Jews. When the king realized how evil and deceptive Haman was, he became furious.

▶ Note **Esther 7:10**. What eventually happens to Haman?

_____

_____

▶ Finally, note **Esther 8:11** and **9:16**. Thanks to the king's help, what can the Jews do?

_____

_____

Possessing the Land

God often keeps His promises by working behind the scenes. He works through all kinds of people—but most importantly, He works through people courageous enough to follow Him.

▶ Choose one of the following passages and explain why Esther or Mordecai needed courage in that situation.

Esther 2:8–11	Esther 2:16–18	Esther 2:21–23	Esther 3:1–4	Esther 4:1–8	Esther 5:1–8	Esther 7:1–6

_____

_____

_____

_____

_____

_____

▶ Name three kinds of fear that can discourage us from doing the right thing.

◉ _____

_____

◉ _____

_____

◉ _____

_____

The Suffering of Job

Vocabulary

- **Suffering** – The hardship felt during times of pain or loss

- **Upright** – Another word meaning *righteous* or *just*

- **Conform** – To become like someone or something

27-A Satan's Plan

We face many troubles in this world. Sometimes we hurt because of sin that we committed. Since God loves us, He will correct us. He lets us see the consequences of doing wrong. But sometimes we suffer even when doing the right thing. This is what happened to a man named Job.

▶ Job probably lived around the time of Abraham. To find out more, read **Job 1:1–5** and fill in the blanks below:

⊙ Job lived in the land of _____. He was a righteous man who feared God and rejected evil. (v. 1)

⊙ He had _____ sons and _____ daughters. (v. 2)

⊙ He had many animals, including _____ sheep and _____ camels. He also had many workers. (v. 3)

⊙ For his children's sake, he often made burnt _____ to God. (v. 5)

Job had a good life. He followed God, and God blessed him. But bad things often happen to good people. Would Job keep trusting God if his life seemed terrible? Someone wanted to find out.

► Job's character caught Satan's attention. Continue reading in **Job 1:6–12** and answer the following:

⊙ According to Satan, why does Job obey God? (vv. 9–10)

_____

_____

⊙ What does Satan think that Job will do if God takes everything away? (v. 11)

_____

► God allows Job to endure this trial. In just one day, his life fell apart. Read the verses below and list what he lost.

Job 1:13–15	
Job 1:16	
Job 1:17	
Job 1:18–19	

⊙ Look at **Job 1:22**. Does Job sin during all this? ☐ Yes ☐ No

► Satan still claimed he could make Job curse God. Read **Job 2:3–10** and answer the following:

⊙ What is Satan allowed to do next? (v. 7)

_____

_____

⊙ At this point, what does Job's wife tell him to do? (v. 9)

_____

⊙ But after all this, does Job say anything sinful? (v. 10) ☐ Yes ☐ No

► What character traits has Job shown in the story so far?

_____

_____

_____

27-B Job's Suffering

Job did not know why God allowed him to face all these bad things. As he sat wondering, a few friends came to support him during this hard time. They wept for him and sat with him for seven days without saying anything.

▶ Then Job finally spoke. In **Job 3:1–3** and **11**, what does he do?

_____

_____

Job's friends could not stand to hear this. So they tried to make sense out of Job's suffering. They tried to explain why so many bad things had happened.

▶ What did Job and his friends talk about? Read the following passages and complete the summaries.

What Job's Friends Thought	What Job Thought
Eliphaz | Job 4:7–8	**Job 6:24**
Has an _____ person ever perished? People reap the bad things they sow.	_____ me, and I will not say anything. Help me understand what I did wrong.
Bildad | Job 8:5–6	**Job 9:15**
If you are _____ and **upright**, God will restore your home when you ask.	I am _____, but I still cannot answer God.
Zophar | Job 11:14–15	**Job 12:6**
Put away the _____ in your hand, and you will not fear.	Even bad people do well sometimes. Sinners can prosper like the righteous.

Job's friends thought that Job must have done something wrong. Job kept claiming that he was innocent. He wanted to argue his case before God—to ask why God had allowed these terrible things.

After a long time, Job's youngest friend Elihu spoke up. He said that God would not do anything wicked. If bad things happened, God must have allowed them for a good purpose. God turns evil toward good, even if we don't understand it right away. Job was foolish to think that God viewed him like an enemy.

▶ Read what Elihu says in **Job 36:24–33**. Does he think we can fully understand God?
☐ Yes ☐ No

▶ Read what Elihu says in **Job 37:14–20**. Can we teach God anything?
☐ Yes ☐ No

27-C God's Answer

We often don't know why God lets us suffer. We can't understand all of God's plans. He has so much more wisdom and knowledge than we do. That's why He asks us to have faith in Him.

▶ After Job's long debate with his friends, God began to speak. What does He ask Job in **Job 38:4**?

_____

_____

God spoke from a whirlwind. He did not say that Job had sinned, nor did He tell Job that all the suffering was a test. Instead, God described the wonders of creation. He talked about the mysteries of animals like the horse, the hawk, and other powerful creatures. In Job 41, God describes a gigantic beast called Leviathan that would terrify Job if it came close.

God had formed everything—the animals, the earth, and even the stars. How could anyone challenge His wisdom or power?

▶ Read **Job 42:1–6**. How did Job feel after seeing and hearing God in the whirlwind?

_____

_____

_____

▶ What happened to Job after all this? Read **Job 42:7–17** and answer the following questions.

⊙ Why is God angry with Eliphaz, Bildad, and Zophar? (v. 7)

_____

_____

⊙ What does God do for Job? (v. 10)

_____

_____

_____

⊙ Do you believe Job still had faith in God after all this? Why or why not?

_____

_____

_____

Possessing the Land

God did not tell Job why he suffered. Job spent the rest of his life without a clear answer. But in Scripture, we learn more about why God allows bad things to happen.

▶ Read the passages below and mark the best answer for each question.

⊙ **Romans 8:28** – What does God work all things toward?

☐ **nothing** ☐ **the harmony of the universe** ☐ **the good of those who love God**

⊙ **1 Corinthians 10:13** – When we are tempted, what does God give us?

☐ **a way to escape** ☐ **perfect happiness** ☐ **an excuse to sin**

⊙ **Psalm 46:1, 7, 11** – How does this psalm describe God?

☐ **a well-defended place** ☐ **a whirlwind** ☐ **a sky full of stars**

▶ It's important to ask questions, but we will not know all the answers until we reach heaven. Read the questions below. Mark the questions that you think **can** be answered in this life.

☐	What can I learn from my mistakes? How can I avoid failing like that again?
☐	Why did God make me the way He did? How does that glorify Him?
☐	What are all the consequences of my actions?
☐	How can I help people who suffer in the same way I have?
☐	Why does God allow any suffering at all?

▶ Think of one difficult thing that you're facing right now. How can you trust and obey God, even through this?

_____

_____

_____

_____

LESSON 28
Songs of Praise

Vocabulary

- **Psalm** – A sacred song or poem

- **Psalmist** – A person who writes a psalm

- **Chaff** – The empty husks left behind after threshing grain

- **Cornerstone** – The first or most important stone laid down for a building

- **Messiah / Christ** – A person anointed or chosen for a special role; the promised Savior Jesus

28-A Songs to God

In the Book of **Psalms** we find beautiful songs of prayer and worship. These were written by different **psalmists** for different reasons. Some are songs of joy and celebration, while others are sad cries of hurt. All of them encourage us to praise God and tell Him what we feel.

▶ Read the following passages and match them to what the psalmist does in those verses. Each answer will be used only once.

	Psalm 8:1	
	Psalm 22:19–21	**A.** Describing God's glory
		B. Thanking God
	Psalm 38:1–5	**C.** Crying for help
	Psalm 95:1–2	**D.** Repenting from sin
		E. Remembering history
	Psalm 136:10–16	

▶ In **Psalm 1**, the psalmist compares two types of people—the *righteous* and the *unrighteous*. The words draw pictures of these two kinds of people. Read the psalm and answer the questions.

⊙ In your own words, what does the "blessed" person *not* do? (v. 1)

_____

_____

⊙ Instead, what does this person do? (v. 2)

_____

_____

⊙ What is the righteous person like? (v. 3)

_____

_____

⊙ But what are the wicked like? (v. 4)

_____

▶ Think about how the psalmist describes the righteous and the wicked. What do you think is the big idea of Psalm 1?

_____

_____

28-B Psalms Fulfilled by Jesus

▶ Some of the psalms hint at the future, including the life of Jesus. Read the verses from Psalms, and then match them to their "echoes" in the New Testament.

	Prophecy in Psalms	New Testament Passage
	Psalm 22:1	**A. Matthew 21:42–44** Even though people rejected Him, Jesus became the **cornerstone** of God's plan.
	Psalm 22:18	**B. Matthew 27:46** On the cross, Jesus cried out to God.
	Psalm 110:4	**C. John 19:24** While Jesus suffered, soldiers gambled over His clothing.
	Psalm 118:22	**D. Hebrews 6:20** Jesus is a priest like Melchizedek in the Old Testament.

Throughout the Old Testament are messages about the coming **Messiah**. He would be a deliverer, a person anointed to rescue God's people from trouble. Most Jews thought that the Messiah would free Israel from the foreign nations who oppressed them. But Jesus had an even more important task—to save the world from sin and judgment.

▶ **Psalm 2** is another that describes God's "anointed." Read the psalm and mark the correct ending to each sentence below.

Verses 1–3: The kings of the earth stand together just so they can . . .

☐ rebel against God.   ☐ have peace.   ☐ worship God.

Verse 4: God responds to their actions by . . .

☐ praising them.   ☐ becoming afraid.   ☐ laughing at their effort.

Verses 7–9: God will help His Son . . .

☐ flee with Israel from the rebellious kings.   ☐ build a palace in Zion.   ☐ break the nations that rebel against Him.

Verses 10–12: The psalmist tells the kings that they should be wise and . . .

☐ respect the Lord.   ☐ try to hide from God.   ☐ gather their armies.

28-C Meditating on Scripture

When we meditate on Scripture, we keep God's Word in our thoughts. We read His truth again and again, connecting it to every corner of our mind. As we spend time in study and meditation, God will use His words to grow us.

▶ Read **Deuteronomy 6:4–6**. Here Moses tells the Israelites about their covenant with God. God wants His people to know His Law so that they will obey it and live peacefully in the promised land. Complete the following.

⊚ Moses says that the Lord our God is _____. (v. 4)

⊚ Because there are no other gods, how should the people love God? (v. 5)

With all their _____

With all their _____

And with all their _____

⊚ What is one big way the people could show their love? (v. 6)

_____

_____

► How could the people keep God's words close? Continue reading in **Deuteronomy 6:7-9** and complete the summaries below.

Verse 7	The people should pass God's Word on to their _____. They should talk about His Law all throughout the day.
Verse 8	They should _____ His words on their hands and foreheads.
Verse 9	They should write His words on the _____ of their houses, as well as on their gates.

► If the people did everything above, would it be easy to forget God's Word? Why or why not?

_____

_____

► Read **Psalm 119:97-104** and answer the following questions.

⊙ What does the psalmist spend the day meditating on? (v. 97) _____

⊙ What does the psalmist gain from God's commands? (vv. 98-99)

_____

⊙ After spending time in God's Word, what does the psalmist hate? (v. 104)

_____

Possessing the Land

► Write a short poem or song to God. You might praise Him for who He is, thank Him for what He does, or ask Him for help. Use another sheet of paper, if needed.

_____

_____

_____

_____

_____

_____

_____

_____

_____

LESSON 29
Wisdom and Vanity

Vocabulary

- **The Fear of the Lord** – Respect and reverence for God

- **Fool** – A person who refuses to learn; in Scripture, someone who does not fear God

- **Ecclesiastes** – Preacher; from the Greek word *ekklesiastes*

- **Vanity** – Something that is vain, worthless, meaningless, or futile; empty pride

29-A The Source of Wisdom

The Book of Proverbs is about the value of God's wisdom. The book includes a wealth of sayings that can teach us deep, spiritual truths. Many of the proverbs were written by King Solomon, but some were written by other people.

▶ Read **Proverbs 1:1–7**. These verses explain what the Book of Proverbs is for.

◉ In your own words, what does Solomon promise to people who study this book? (vv. 2–6)

_____

_____

_____

God wants His truth to fill our minds and flow through our actions. If we truly understand God's wisdom, we will live it out. We will treat other people with care and respect, and we will face our problems with knowledge and discernment.

◉ What attitude is the beginning of knowledge? (v. 7)

_____

◉ On the other hand, what do **fools** do? (v. 7)

_____

► Read **Proverbs 2:1–8** and complete the following summaries.

Verse 4	Solomon encourages people to search for wisdom like they might search for hidden _____.
Verse 5	If we truly search for wisdom, we will understand the fear of the Lord and find the _____.
Verse 6	We know this because the Lord gives _____.
Verse 7	He stores up _____ for those who do right.
Verse 7	He is a _____ to those who walk the right way.
Verse 8	He _____ the way walked by His own.

► Look again at **Proverbs 1:7** and **2:6**. Why would fearing God help us be wise?

_____

_____

_____

29-B The Beauty of Wisdom

The proverbs in Scripture often compare a wise person with a fool. The wise person seeks out truth, but the foolish person remains ignorant. The wise person is no smarter than a fool, but wisdom helps everyone use their knowledge well.

► Read the following passages. Describe the wise person in contrast to the foolish person.

Passage	Wise people . . .	But fools . . .
Proverbs 3:35		
Proverbs 10:8		
Proverbs 12:15		

Passage	Wise people . . .	But fools . . .
Proverbs 14:16		
Proverbs 21:20		
Proverbs 29:11		

▶ Draw a comic that compares a wise person to a foolish person. Come up with your own topic, or choose one from below:

- ⊙ How do they study?

- ⊙ How do they treat others?

- ⊙ Who do they ask for advice?

The Wise Person	The Foolish Person

29-C A Life of Wisdom

The Book of *Ecclesiastes* asks a few difficult but important questions. Maybe the biggest question is this: "What should be the goal of my life?"

► How would you answer this question?

_____

_____

You may already know a good answer. A lot of people do, but they don't *live* like they know the answer. They spend their time on things that will not last.

► The writer of Ecclesiastes lists many things that people value. But over time, the writer has found all of these things to be empty and useless. Read each passage below and write what is **vanity**.

Ecclesiastes 1:2	
Ecclesiastes 1:16–17	
Ecclesiastes 2:1	
Ecclesiastes 2:17	
Ecclesiastes 5:10	

Many people build their entire lives around these things. They work hard to find some kind of happiness, but none of it lasts.

► Read **Ecclesiastes 3:1–8** and list six of the things that God has allowed time for.

There's a time to . . .	And a time to . . .

No matter what we do, the world keeps on going. People live and die. We dance and mourn. Wars begin and end. Leaders rise up and fall. As we grow up, we learn how to face these times gracefully. But is there anything that *doesn't* change?

God is eternal, and He sees everything across eternity. His wisdom is greater than ours. Nothing lasts without Him. So we must look to God for our goal or purpose.

▶ Read **Ecclesiastes 3:14** and answer the following questions.

⊙ How long does God's work last? _____

⊙ Can anyone change what God does? ☐ Yes ☐ No

⊙ What attitude should we have toward Him? _____

▶ Even if we don't become rich or famous, how can we have a meaningful life? At the end of the book, the writer explains the path we should take. Read **Ecclesiastes 12:13–14** and answer the following questions.

⊙ What is our duty? (v. 13)

_____

_____

⊙ Why should we do this? (v. 14)

_____

_____

Possessing the Land

▶ Think about the wisdom you use from day to day. Mark your answers to the questions below.

When I receive money, I usually . . .	☐ Spend it all right away.
	☐ Give some to God and save some.
	☐ Save it all for myself.
When I talk with my friends, I often . . .	☐ Say whatever pops into my head.
	☐ Try to say something true and helpful.
	☐ Say nothing.
After learning about God's commands, I usually . . .	☐ Forget about them.
	☐ Try to remember and do them.
When I feel angry, I . . .	☐ Lose my temper and lash out at others.
	☐ Try not to hurt others while I deal with the anger.
When someone gives me good advice, I . . .	☐ Ignore it and do what I think is best.
	☐ Think about it.

LESSON 30
Three Prophets

Vocabulary

- **Vision** – Seeing something; in Scripture, a glimpse of something supernatural or divine

- **Seraph / Seraphim** – Angelic beings with six wings

- **Idolatry** – The practice of worshiping idols or false gods

- **Potter** – A person who makes pots, often by shaping clay

- **Sanctuary** – A safe place, protected from harm; a sacred place blessed by God

- **Abomination** – Something that is utterly disgusting; in Scripture, a terrible sin that God hates

30-A Isaiah

Around 586 BC, the Babylonians conquered the southern kingdom of Judah. Long before this happened, the event was predicted by the prophet Isaiah. He warned the people about God's judgment, but they would not repent or even listen to him.

▶ Read **Isaiah 1:2-4**. Explain in your own words what was wrong in Judah.

_____

_____

▶ When God called Isaiah to be a prophet, He gave the man a startling **vision** of heaven's throne room. Read **Isaiah 6:1-8** and answer the following questions.

⊙ Who is sitting on the throne? (v. 1) _____

⊙ How do the **seraphim** describe Him? (v. 3)

_____

⊙ After seeing all this, how does Isaiah describe himself? (v. 5)

_____

◉ What happens to Isaiah when the seraphim touches his lips with a hot coal? (vv. 6–7)

_____

_____

◉ When the Lord asks for someone to send, what does Isaiah say? (v. 8)

_____

Isaiah's ministry would be very difficult. God knew that Judah would not listen to Isaiah, but the prophet needed to speak anyway. There would be at least a few believers in Judah who would follow God.

▶ Continue reading what God says in **Isaiah 6:9–13** and answer the following questions.

◉ What will happen to the land? (v. 11)

_____

_____

◉ What does God use to picture the few people who remain and obey Him? (v. 13)

_____

Because of Judah's ***idolatry***, the Babylonians would one day conquer the land. But the city of Babylon worshiped idols, as well. How could God use a sinful nation to punish Judah? That didn't seem fair.

▶ God would not ignore Babylon's sin, either. Read **Isaiah 13:19–22**. What will happen to Babylon?

_____

_____

_____

_____

_____

_____

God would judge any nation that rejected Him. When the people of Israel chose to sin, they chose to join God's enemies and face the same kind of punishment.

Still, God would continue looking after His people. He would not allow them to be wiped off the face of the earth. He would preserve those who followed Him. As we read in Ezra and Nehemiah, God eventually led His people back from captivity to the promised land.

30-B Jeremiah

Jeremiah lived in Judah just before—and during—the Babylonian conquest. Like the prophet Isaiah, he warned the people about their sin and God's judgment.

One day, God told Jeremiah to visit the house of a **potter**. There the prophet learned something about the relationship between God and His people.

► Read **Jeremiah 18:1–12** and then mark the following statements as true or false. If a statement is false, re-write it correctly in the space below.

☐ True ☐ False	**Verses 3–4** – The potter's first creation is perfect.
Correction: _____

☐ True ☐ False	**Verse 6** – God says that Israel is like the potter.
Correction: _____

☐ True ☐ False	**Verses 7–8** – If a nation turns from its evil, God will not destroy it like He said.
Correction: _____

☐ True ☐ False	**Verses 9–10** – God will continue building up a nation even if it does evil in His sight.
Correction: _____

☐ True ☐ False	**Verse 11** – Jeremiah should tell the people to turn from evil.
Correction: _____

☐ True ☐ False	**Verse 12** – God says that the people will listen to Jeremiah and repent from their sin.
Correction: _____ _____	

God did not punish His people to be cruel. He loved Israel and Judah very much. Most of the people had rejected God, along with His protection and blessing. The people had disobeyed, so they could blame themselves for the consequences.

► The people did not listen to Jeremiah, and God allowed them to be taken captive by Babylon. But what promise does God make to them in **Jeremiah 29:10**?

_____

_____

► Finally, continue reading **Jeremiah 29:11–14**. What is God's attitude toward the people of Israel? Check every word that you think applies.

☐ Angry	☐ Loving	☐ Cruel	☐ Caring	☐ Attentive	☐ Near	☐ Distant	☐ Selfish

30-C Ezekiel

Ezekiel began life in Judah but was taken captive along with his people. Even in captivity, he found a purpose. God chose him to preach to the other Jews in Babylon. Ezekiel warned them about their idolatry, reminding them that God still saw their actions.

God also gave Ezekiel another message: the Jews would see their home in Israel again. Ezekiel encouraged the captives with the hope that God would bring them back. God had not forgotten His promises to them.

► Read **Ezekiel 11:14–21** and complete the following.

Verse 15	The people now living in the city of _____ have pushed away the Israelites and claimed the land for themselves.
Verse 16	The Lord is still a _____ for the Jews scattered among other nations.
Verse 17	God will gather them and give them back the land of _____.
Verse 18	The Jews will then get rid of all the _____ _____.

Verses 19–20	God will give the people a new _____ so that they will follow Him and keep His commands.
Verse 20	They will be His _____, and He will be their _____.
Verse 21	But as for people who keep following evil, God will bring the consequences for sin down on their heads.

Possessing the Land

► Read the following passages and write the command that God gave each prophet.

⊙ **Isaiah 6:9** – _____

_____

⊙ **Jeremiah 1:7** – _____

_____

⊙ **Ezekiel 2:4** – _____

_____

God gave His messengers a serious and difficult job. The message was important, but the people did not want to hear it. It would have been easy for the prophets to say whatever the people wanted, but they needed God's truth, instead.

God wants Christians today to speak His message, too. People don't always want the truth, but we should offer it with love and care.

► Choose one of the situations below and explain how you could offer the truth lovingly.

1. Your brother thinks that you spilled tea all over his homework, but you didn't.

2. Your classmate thinks that studying science is a waste of time.

3. Your friend thinks that God is cruel for allowing her mother to get sick.

_____

_____

_____

_____

_____

_____

Vocabulary

- **Discipline** – Self-control; training to do what is good, healthy, and right

- **Defile** – To make filthy or corrupt

- **Herald** – To declare a message, often for a king; also a name for someone who heralds

31-A Far from Home

As a young man, Daniel was captured and taken to live in Babylon. While there, he faced hardship and the pressure to disobey God. His captors didn't obey God or even believe God existed. Daniel needed courage to stand for what was right, especially when God's enemies threatened him with death.

► Read **Daniel 1:1–7** and answer the following questions.

◉ When the Babylonian king Nebuchadnezzar conquers Jerusalem, who does he choose to bring back to Babylon? (vv. 3–4)

_____

_____

◉ What does Nebuchadnezzar want to do with them? (v. 5)

_____

◉ These young people are taken from their homeland and given new names. Look at **verse 7** and write the Babylonian names for Daniel and his three friends below.

Daniel:	**Mishael:**
Hananiah:	**Azariah:**

► Continue reading in **Daniel 1:8–17** and mark the correct ending to each of the following sentences.

Verse 8: When offered food that was forbidden by the Law, Daniel chooses . . .

☐ not to **defile** himself with the food.

☐ to **defile** himself with the food.

☐ to **defile** the food by adding pineapple to it.

Verse 8: Daniel is a prisoner, so he tries to solve his problem by. . .

☐ demanding better food.

☐ asking for permission not to eat the food.

☐ hiding the food under his bed.

Verses 9–10: The official is nervous about helping Daniel because . . .

☐ the king expects the Jewish captives to stay healthy.

☐ the cook might get offended and angry.

☐ he thinks the Jewish rules are foolish.

Verses 11–13: When Daniel understands what everyone wants, he . . .

☐ asks for servants to go gather food from Israel.

☐ decides to starve himself for ten days.

☐ asks for a test to see who will look healthier.

Verse 15: At the end of this time, Daniel and his friends . . .

☐ are dead.

☐ are pale and sick.

☐ look much healthier.

Verse 17: As Daniel and his friends grow up, God gives them . . .

☐ skill in battle.

☐ many kinds of wisdom and understanding.

☐ great wealth.

31-B A Voice for God

▶ Read **Daniel 2:1–18** and match each question on the left with the correct answer on the right.

	What does King Nebuchadnezzar command all his advisors to do? (vv. 3–5)	**A.** Pray to God for mercy so that they would live
	What do the advisors ask the king to do? (vv. 4, 7)	**B.** Describe what he dreamed *and* explain what the dream means
	When the advisors cannot help Nebuchadnezzar, what does he decide to do? (vv. 5, 12–13)	**C.** Talk to them and ask for a time to meet the king
	What does Daniel have the wisdom to do when the soldiers come to kill him? (vv. 14–16)	**D.** Execute all the wise men in Babylon
	What did Daniel ask his friends to do? (v. 18)	**E.** Describe what he dreamed

God answered their prayers and showed Daniel both the dream and its meaning. The dream was actually a message from God, and God wanted Daniel to explain it.

▶ Read about the dream in **Daniel 2:31–36**. Label what each part of the statue is made from, and then draw your version of the statue.

	Part	Material	Nation
	Head	**Verse 32**	Babylonians
	Chest and Arms	**Verse 32**	Medes & Persians
	Stomach and Thighs	**Verse 32**	Greeks
	Legs or Calves	**Verse 33**	Romans
	Feet	**Verse 33**	Romans Divided

The parts of the statue represented the nations that would come after Babylon. Each would rise after the next, but all of them would fall to the rock that became a mountain. Christians believe that this rock is Jesus Christ, whose spiritual kingdom will never end.

31-C A Test of Worship

Daniel and his three friends trusted God, and God gave them wisdom and favor with the king. Nebuchadnezzar put them all in important positions. Daniel himself took charge of the king's advisors.

The friends would still face difficulties. Nebuchadnezzar believed that Jehovah was the God of all gods, but the king still worshiped other gods, as well. He didn't think that God was the only true God. Even worse, Nebuchadnezzar thought that he, the king, should also be worshiped.

▶ Read **Daniel 3:1–18** and answer the following questions.

⊙ What does the **herald** say will happen to those who do not worship the statue? (vv. 4–6)

_____

⊙ Who attends the ceremony but does *not* worship? (v. 12)

_____

⊙ When Nebuchadnezzar threatens to throw them in the furnace, how do they reply? Explain their answer in your own words. (vv. 16–18)

_____

_____

_____

▶ Continue reading in **Daniel 3:19–30** and number the following events in order from **1** to **7**.

	The king tells several strong soldiers to tie up Meshach, Shadrach, and Abednego and throw them into the furnace.
	The angry king orders the furnace to be heated seven times hotter than usual.
	Looking into the furnace, the king sees four people walking around, not just three.
	The king decrees that no one can speak against God. If they do, they and their houses will be destroyed.
	Meshach, Shadrach, and Abednego come out of the furnace completely unburned. They don't even smell like smoke.
	The king tells the three men to come out of the furnace.
	The soldiers who tie up the three men are killed by the heat from the furnace.

Possessing the Land

Daniel and his friends remained loyal to God during some very difficult times. They had been taken away from their families and moved to a foreign country. Many of their own people rejected God and no longer worshiped Him. It would have been very easy to do what others were doing—to worship Babylonian gods and to follow their customs.

As God blessed Daniel and his friends, they continued to stand for what was right. Even when they received promotions and rewards, they did not live for pleasure. They continued to honor and obey God. They had the discipline to follow Him during the bad times and the good.

▶ In what ways do your friends encourage you to do good?

_____

_____

_____

▶ In what ways do your friends sometimes encourage you to do bad?

_____

_____

_____

▶ Think about one area of your life where you have trouble controlling yourself. What are some ways you can build up discipline or control yourself better?

_____

_____

_____

_____

_____

_____

LESSON 32
Daniel's Devotion

Vocabulary

- **Signet** – A ring used to sign or seal official documents, often for kings and rulers

32-A Writing on the Wall

Later in the book of Daniel, we find him serving under the Babylonian king Belshazzar. This king did not follow God like Nebuchadnezzar had learned to do. Belshazzar was very wicked, and he was the last king of Babylon before the Persians conquered the city.

▶ Read **Daniel 5:1–17** and fill in the following blanks.

Belshazzar invited a _____ of his nobles and rulers to a great
verse 1

banquet. They drank wine from gold and silver cups that had been stolen from God's Temple

in _____. The guests praised the _____ made
verses 2–3 **verse 4**

from gold, silver, bronze, wood, and stone.

Suddenly, Belshazzar saw the _____ of a hand appear and write on
verse 5

the _____ near him. The king was terrified so badly that he grew pale and his
verse 5

_____ shook against each other.
verse 6

The king immediately called all of his advisors. He told them that he would reward

whoever could _____ this writing and explain it. Belshazzar would clothe him
verse 7

in _____, give him a _____ of gold, and make
verse 7 **verse 7**

him the _____ most powerful ruler in the kingdom. But no one could
verse 7

understand the writing on the wall.

The _____ spoke up and said that Daniel could help. He was
verse 10–12

brought quickly, and he said that he would read the writing but not accept any rewards.

▶ Read what Daniel said in **Daniel 5:22–23**. In your own words, what had Belshazzar done wrong?

_____

_____

▶ Continue reading in **Daniel 5:24–28** and complete the summary of each word's meaning.

	Word	Meaning
Verse 26	**MENE**	God has _____ how long Belshazzar would rule and has ended his reign.
Verse 27	**TEKEL**	The king has been weighed and found _____.
Verse 28	**PERES**	His kingdom is _____ and given to the Medes and the Persians.

Belshazzar gave Daniel everything he had promised, but it was an empty reward. That night, the king was killed, and a new king named Darius began to rule over Babylon.

32-B God Saves Daniel

▶ Read **Daniel 6** and match the beginning of each sentence below with the best ending.

	Darius, the new king, appoints 120 officials to . . .	**A.** Set Daniel over the whole realm.
	Because Daniel rules so well, Darius plans to . . .	**B.** Find some complaint or fault with Daniel.
	The other officials try and fail to . . .	**C.** Pray to anyone but the king for 30 days.
	The officials realize that they can only attack Daniel if they . . .	**D.** Close the lions' mouths.
	To trap Daniel, the officials convince the king to make a law punishing people who would . . .	**E.** Change a law already sealed with the royal **signet** ring.
	Despite the new law, Daniel chooses to . . .	**F.** Accuse him of keeping the law of his God.
	Darius is upset to hear that Daniel broke the law, but he cannot . . .	**G.** Pray three times a day, just like before.
	God protects Daniel by sending an angel to . . .	**H.** Execute those who tried to have Daniel killed.
	The king commands that the lions be used to . . .	**I.** Rule over the kingdom.
	The king decrees that everyone in the kingdom should . . .	**J.** Fear the God of Daniel.

32-C Daniel's Faith

▶ Read the following passages and complete the crossword puzzle.

Across

2. Daniel 5:22
Daniel said that Belshazzar had not ____ his heart before God.

7. Daniel 2:27–28
God revealed to Daniel the ____ of King Nebuchadnezzar along with its meaning.

8. Daniel 6:22
God protected Daniel from being eaten by ____.

9. Daniel 2:47
Nebuchadnezzar realized that God was a ____ of mysterious things.

Down

1. Daniel 3:23–26
God protected Meshach, Shadrach, and Abednego when they were thrown into a ____.

3. Daniel 6:20
King Darius called Daniel a servant of the ____ God.

4. Daniel 1:8
Daniel did not ____ himself by disobeying God's rules.

5. Daniel 1:17
God gave Daniel the ability to understand ____ and dreams.

6. Daniel 2:17–18
Daniel and his friends asked the God of ____ to help them.

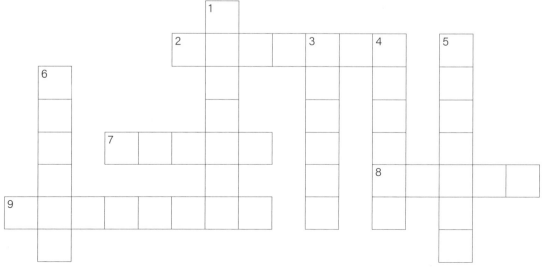

Possessing the Land

Many of the Jews in captivity turned away from God. But Daniel and his friends did not take that easy path. They made difficult choices and faced the consequences. Thankfully, God protected them and blessed their faith. He stayed close to them during these hard times.

► How do you show dedication to God? Mark each statement below from **1** (rarely) to **5** (often).

	Rarely		Sometimes		Often
When my friends want me to do something I know is wrong, I do it to avoid trouble and get them to like me.	1	2	3	4	5
When others are looking, I do what I should. When I'm alone, I don't.	1	2	3	4	5
When I know I'm not supposed to do something, but everybody else is doing it, I'll just go along.	1	2	3	4	5
Other people need to remind or push me to finish my own work.	1	2	3	4	5
When someone praises me for doing a good job, I take all the credit for myself, even if someone else helped me.	1	2	3	4	5
When I see others insulting and pushing someone, I don't say anything or get help from an adult.	1	2	3	4	5

If any of these statements describe you, take a moment to talk to God about it. Ask Him to help you grow more loyal to Him.

Vocabulary

- **Lots** – Items thrown to decide something by chance; often coins, rocks, or sticks

- **Sackcloth** – Rough fabric used for sacks or bags; in Scripture, often worn to show sadness

With only four short chapters, the Book of Jonah is one of the smallest books in the Old Testament. But through Jonah's life, we learn something very important about God. Our heavenly Father offers mercy and love to anyone.

33-A God's Mission for Jonah

▶ Read **Jonah 1:1–3** and answer the following questions.

⊙ What does God tell Jonah to do? (v. 2)

_____

_____

⊙ Why does Jonah need to go to these people? (v. 2)

_____

⊙ But what does Jonah do? (v. 3)

_____

_____

▶ Continue reading in **Jonah 1:4–17** and fill in the following blanks:

As the ship sailed toward Tarshish, God sent a great _____, and the sea
                                                                    verse 4

grew stormy. It seemed like the ship was going to _____. The
                                                                    verse 4

men on the ship felt _____ and cried out to their own _____.
                          verse 5   **verse 5**

To keep the ship from sinking, they threw things overboard.

Meanwhile, Jonah was _____. The ship's captain woke him and told

_{verse 5}

him to call on his _____ to save them. Then the men cast _____

_{verse 6} _{verse 7}

to find out who was to blame for the storm. It fell on _____.

_{verse 7}

After the sailors found out what Jonah had done, they asked him what they could do to

calm the sea. Jonah told them to _____ him up and _____

_{verse 12} _{verse 12}

him into the sea. The men did not want to, so they tried rowing back to _____

_{verse 13}

—but the sea became even worse.

Finally, after begging God not to punish them, they threw Jonah overboard. Soon after,

the sea _____. The sailors offered a

_{verse 15}

sacrifice to God. The Lord also chose a big _____ to _____

_{verse 17} _{verse 17}

Jonah. He stayed there for _____ days and _____ nights.

_{verse 17} _{verse 17}

33-B God's Message for Nineveh

▶ Read **Jonah 2:1–9**. What does Jonah do while inside the fish?

_____

_____

▶ What happens in **Jonah 2:10**?

_____

_____

▶ Read **Jonah 3:1–5** and answer the following.

⊙ Does God change His mind about sending Jonah to Nineveh? (v. 2) ☐ Yes ☐ No

⊙ This time, does Jonah obey God's command? (v. 3) ☐ Yes ☐ No

⊙ What message does Jonah declare in the city? Use your own words. (v. 4)

_____

_____

⊙ Did the Ninevites believe God's message? (v. 5) ☐ Yes ☐ No

▶ Continue reading in **Jonah 3:6–9**. What did the king of Nineveh command the people to do?

Verse 7	Do not let anyone _____.
Verse 8	Cover all people and animals with _____.
Verse 8	_____ to God.
Verse 8	Turn from their _____ ways and _____.

▶ Finally, read **Jonah 3:10**. How did God respond to the Ninevites' repentance?

_____

_____

33-C God's Mercy for All

▶ Think about the story in Jonah so far. Read each statement below and mark if it describes Jonah, the Ninevites, both, or neither.

	Jonah	The Ninevites
Always did the right thing	☐	☐
Sinned	☐	☐
Received a message from God	☐	☐
Obeyed God's command right away after hearing it	☐	☐
Repented and prayed to God	☐	☐
Received mercy from God	☐	☐

▶ Jonah was not happy about the Ninevites' repentance. Read **Jonah 4** and answer the following.

⊙ What does Jonah accuse God of being? (v. 2)

_____

_____

◉ What does God use to teach Jonah about mercy? (vv. 5–8)

_____

_____

_____

Possessing the Land

If Jonah tried to see the Ninevites from God's point of view, he might have been able to love them. It is difficult to love others when we focus on our own fears and pain.

▶ Think about someone you know who is difficult to love. Why is it difficult to show love to this person?

_____

_____

_____

▶ How do you think God views this person?

_____

_____

▶ With God's help, how might you better show love to this person?

_____

_____

_____

_____

Vocabulary

- **Remnant** – Something or someone that remains; what is left over

The prophetic books in the Old Testament are divided into the *Major Prophets* and the *Minor Prophets*. The major prophets are not more important—they simply wrote longer books than the minor prophets did. Most of the minor prophetic books are very short.

The Four Major Prophets			
Isaiah	Jeremiah	Ezekiel	Daniel

The Twelve Minor Prophets					
Hosea	Joel	Amos	Obadiah	Jonah	Micah
Nahum	Habakkuk	Zephaniah	Haggai	Zechariah	Malachi

34-A Hosea, Joel, Amos, Obadiah

Hosea

Hosea was a prophet to the northern kingdom of Israel. He pleaded with the people to stop worshiping idols and instead turn back to God. He prophesied right up until the Assyrians captured the kingdom.

▶ Even Hosea's family pictures God's message. Read what God told the prophet in **Hosea 1:3–10**. How will the prophet's children carry God's message?

_____

_____

When Hosea's wife left him and got into trouble, the prophet rescued her. Even this was a picture of God's love. God rescued Israel even after the nation rejected Him many times.

Joel

The Book of Joel doesn't say when the prophet's ministry took place. Joel prophesies about the people of Judah and the city of Jerusalem, so he probably served there.

▶ Read **Joel 2:12–13**. What does God want the people to do?

_____

_____

▶ Note **verse 13** again. Write at least three words or phrases that Joel uses to describe God.

◉ _____

◉ _____

◉ _____

Amos

Amos was a shepherd, but God called him to serve as a prophet. He gave God's messages to the northern kingdom of Israel.

▶ Read **Amos 5:12**. In addition to idolatry, what sins are the people committing?

_____

_____

_____

▶ Read **Amos 5:14–15** and answer the following.

◉ What does God tell the people to seek? _____

◉ What does God tell the people to hate? _____

Obadiah

This short book doesn't explain when or where the prophet lived. Obadiah delivered a message from God to the Edomites, the descendents of Esau. This people did not follow the Lord, and they treated the Israelites badly.

▶ Read **verses 11–14** of Obadiah. What did the Edomites do while Jerusalem and Judah suffered?

_____

_____

▶ Read **verse 15**. What will happen to the Edomites?

_____

_____

34-B Jonah, Micah, Nahum, Habakkuk

▶ Read the following passages and mark the correct ending to each sentence.

Jonah

Jonah 4:10 – At this time, Jonah cares most about . . .

☐ the people of Nineveh.	☐ his own comfort.	☐ the health of the worm.

Jonah 4:11 – God seems to care most about . . .

☐ the people of Nineveh.	☐ Jonah's comfort.	☐ the health of the fish.

Micah

Micah prophesied to Judah during the reign of several kings. This prophet served just before Israel was conquered by Assyria.

Micah 6:6–8 – Instead of sacrifices, God really wants . . .

☐ the people to do right.	☐ every family's firstborn.	☐ the people's money.

Nahum

Like Jonah, Nahum prophesied a message for Nineveh. But this happened at a different time, and unlike Jonah, Nahum did not travel to the city.

Nahum 1:7 – During trouble, God is like a . . .

☐ flood.	☐ great darkness.	☐ stronghold or refuge.

Nahum 1:8–11 – God will judge Nineveh because the Ninevites . . .

☐ betrayed the Israelites.	☐ planned evil things against God.	☐ offered bad sacrifices.

Habakkuk

Habakkuk prophesied to Judah before the kingdom was conquered by the Babylonians (Chaldeans). Most of the passages in this book are poetic.

Habakkuk 1:12–13 – Habbakuk asks the Lord why He allows the wicked . . .

☐ to suffer so much pain.	☐ to exist at all.	☐ to consume someone more righteous.

Habakkuk 2:8 – The Babylonians will suffer because they . . .

☐ hurt and oppressed other nations.	☐ surrendered to other nations.	☐ gave God no other choice.

34-C Zephaniah, Haggai, Zechariah, Malachi

There are just four more prophets left in the Old Testament:

- Zephaniah was the great-grandson of King Hezekiah of Judah. This prophet warned the people of Judah about God's judgment for their idolatry.

- Haggai and Zechariah prophesied around the time of Ezra. They preached to the Jews as they returned from exile and rebuilt the Temple in Jerusalem.

- Malachi prophesied around the time of Nehemiah. Like other prophets, Malachi pointed out the sins of the people, but he did this with a long series of questions and answers. This encouraged the people to think.

▶ Read each summary and match it to the correct passage.

	The people complain that serving God is useless. God explains that He remembers the righteous and spares them from punishment.	**A. Zephaniah 1:4-6**
	God will cut off or destroy every ***remnant*** of Ba'al, along with those who do not follow God.	**B. Haggai 1:9, 12-14**
	God promises that if the people return to Him, He will also return to them.	**C. Zechariah 1:1-3**
	The people are busy building their own houses instead of God's house. But they listen to the prophet and begin rebuilding the Temple.	**D. Malachi 3:13-18**

Possessing the Land

After the exile, the Jews had to ask themselves where their loyalty rested. Did they value God more than anyone or anything else? Would they worship Him instead of power, wealth, or false gods? All the prophets urged the people to follow God once more.

▶ In the spaces below, write five things you believe should be most important to you.

1. _____

2. _____

3. _____

4. _____

5. _____

Does your life reflect this kind of loyalty right now? Take a moment to pray about the way you spend your time and energy.

LESSON 35
Review

35-A Multiple Choice

▶ Choose the best answer to complete the following sentences. For help, check the page numbers.

1. Samuel replaced Eli as a . . . (p. 92)

   A. priest and judge.   **B.** king.   **C.** captain.

2. The Israelites wanted a king so that they could . . . (p. 93)

   A. build a massive empire, from North Africa all the way to East Asia.
   B. have a spiritual leader that was better than priests.
   C. be like the other nations.

3. The first king of Israel was . . . (p. 96)

   A. Samuel.   **B.** Saul.   **C.** Solomon.

4. God took the kingship away from Saul because . . . (pp. 97–98)

   A. he exiled his son Jonathan and assassinated David.
   B. he ignored Samuel and disobeyed God.
   C. he had a violent temper.

5. When God told Saul to destroy the Amalekites and their possessions, he . . . (p. 98)

   A. obeyed God absolutely.
   B. killed only the king of the Amalekites.
   C. destroyed everything but the king and the best animals.

6. God wants ___ more than sacrifice. (p. 99)

   A. obedience   **B.** money   **C.** perfection

7. David believed that he could defeat Goliath because . . . (p. 102)

   A. he had Saul's armor to protect him.
   B. he was stronger and faster.
   C. God had protected him before.

8. David became close friends with Saul's son, whose name was . . . (p. 103)

   A. Jonathan.   **B.** Jehu.   **C.** Josiah.

9. Even though Saul was a bad king, David respected him because Saul was ... (p. 104)

   A. older than David.   **B.** David's father-in-law.   **C.** God's anointed king.

10. God promised David that his kingdom would be ... (p. 108)

    A. small, but perfect.
    B. established from his descendants.
    C. destroyed after one generation.

11. David sinned by taking a census of Israel's fighting men, and then he ... (p. 108)

    A. took a census of everyone else.
    B. repented before God.
    C. went to war.

12. Israel's first three kings, in order, are ... (p. 111)

    A. David, Solomon, and then Saul.
    B. Saul, David, and then Solomon.
    C. David, Saul, and then Solomon.

13. God told Solomon that if he or his sons served or worshiped false gods ... (p. 114)

    A. they would become slaves in Egypt once again.
    B. their kingdom would expand.
    C. God would cut off Israel from the land and destroy the Temple.

14. After Solomon's reign, Israel divided into two kingdoms called ... (p. 117)

    A. Israel and Judah.   **B.** Judah and Moab.   **C.** Judea and Samaria.

15. The ministry of Elijah continued with the prophet named ... (p. 119)

    A. Isaiah.   **B.** Jeremiah.   **C.** Elisha.

16. Ezra helped the Jewish people rebuild the ___ after the exile. (p. 122)

    A. Temple   **B.** walls   **C.** palace

17. The Persian king who allowed many Jews to return to Israel was ... (p. 122)

    A. Cyrus.   **B.** Nebuchadnezzar.   **C.** Nehemiah.

18. Nehemiah helped the Jewish people rebuild the ___ after the exile. (p. 129)

    A. Temple   **B.** walls   **C.** palace

19. A Jewish woman named ___ helped save every Jew in the Persian empire. (p. 136)

    A. Esther   **B.** Ruth   **C.** Rebekah

20. God didn't give Job a complete answer, but Job suffered because ... (p. 140)

    A. he deserved punishment for a great sin.
    B. God allowed him to be tested.
    C. Satan was more powerful than God.

21. Psalm 1 says that a blessed person . . . (p. 145)

   A. blows away like chaff.
   B. walks with sinners.
   C. meditates on God's Law day and night.

22. According to Proverbs, the beginning of wisdom and knowledge is . . . (p. 148)

   A. the fear of the Lord.
   B. memorizing a dictionary.
   C. believing whatever people tell you.

23. The writer of Ecclesiastes said that ___ is our most important duty. (p. 152)

   A. knowledge and wisdom
   B. to fear God and obey Him
   C. pleasure

24. A man named ___ became a prophet during a vision of God on His throne. (p. 153)

   A. Jeremiah   **B.** Isaiah   **C.** Daniel

25. God used a ___ to show Jeremiah how He would guide Israel and Judah. (p. 155)

   A. farmer   **B.** potter   **C.** woodcarver

26. Daniel and his friends obeyed God by not . . . (p. 159)

   A. eating the king's food.
   B. wearing the king's clothes.
   C. speaking the Babylonian or Chaldean language.

27. At different times, God protected Daniel and his three friends from . . . (pp. 161, 164)

   A. death.   **B.** embarrassment.   **C.** illness.

28. The prophet who tried to run away from God by ship was . . . (p. 167)

   A. Elijah.   **B.** Jonah.   **C.** Haggai.

29. The minor prophets begged people to . . . (pp. 171–174)

   A. build a kingdom that would be ready for the Messiah.
   B. make as much money as they could for the Temple.
   C. repent, turn back to God, or face His judgment.

35-B Vocabulary

▶ Write the correct vocabulary word for each definition. If you forget a word, check the page number.

Across	Down
3. The practice of worshiping idols or false gods (p. 153)	**1.** An Old Testament name for many kinds of false gods; can mean "lord" or "ruler" (p. 116)
6. A person anointed or chosen for a special role; an Old Testament name for Jesus Christ (p. 144)	**2.** A wise saying; a short statement that teaches a general principle (p. 111)
8. The ability to use knowledge well; insight and understanding (p. 111)	**4.** God's work through human or natural events (p. 122)
9. A sacred song or poem (p. 144)	**5.** Self-control; training to do what is good, healthy, and right (p. 158)
10. Choosing not to eat, often to focus on praying or some other spiritual activity (p. 133)	**7.** To put oil on someone; shows that the person is chosen for a special purpose (p. 96)
11. To drive out someone from their home country; to banish or separate (p. 122)	**10.** A person who refuses to learn; in Scripture, someone who does not fear God (p. 148)

35-C Who Am I?

▶ Match the following descriptions with the correct person from the Old Testament.

1.	I served Eli at Shiloh until I replaced him as a priest. (p. 92)	**A.** Abraham
2.	Although I was afraid, God called me to be a judge of Israel. (p. 80)	**B.** Achan
3.	God took my kingdom away because I did not obey Him. (pp. 98–99)	**C.** Daniel
4.	I planned to have all the Jews in Persia killed. (p. 135)	**D.** David
5.	To take care of Naomi, I came to Israel from Moab. (p. 82, 85)	**E.** Deborah
6.	I was thrown into a furnace for not worshiping a statue. (p. 161)	**F.** Elijah
7.	I was a prophetess who had leprosy after complaining. (p. 46, 58)	**G.** Elisha
8.	With God's wisdom, I advised at least three kings. (pp. 158–165)	**H.** Esther
9.	Although I led the Israelites, I did not get to enter Canaan. (p. 64)	**I.** Ezekiel
10.	God gave me the chance to build the Temple for Him. (p. 113)	**J.** Ezra
11.	I disobeyed God by stealing some things from Jericho. (p. 75)	**K.** Gideon
12.	Although I was Saul's son, I befriended and helped David. (p. 103)	**L.** Haman
13.	I lost almost everything I had, but I continued to trust God. (p. 140)	**M.** Job
14.	After the exile, I taught God's Law to Jews in Jerusalem. (p. 124)	**N.** Jonah
15.	I convinced the king of Persia not to kill the Jews. (p. 137)	**O.** Jonathan
16.	I asked King Artaxerxes to help the Jews in Jerusalem. (pp. 128–129)	**P.** Joseph
17.	After I prayed, God sent down fire on Mount Carmel. (pp. 118–119)	**Q.** Joshua
18.	I led the early conquest of Canaan. (pp. 67–68)	**R.** Miriam
19.	I trusted God and fought the Philistine champion. (p. 102)	**S.** Moses
20.	God gave me a double portion of Elijah's spirit. (p. 119)	**T.** Nehemiah
21.	God told me I'd have as many descendants as the stars. (p. 17)	**U.** Rahab
22.	I was upset that God showed mercy to the Ninevites. (p. 169)	**V.** Ruth
23.	I was sold into slavery, but became second to Pharaoh. (p. 34)	**W.** Samuel
24.	I helped the Israelite spies escape from Jericho. (p. 72)	**X.** Saul
25.	I was a prophetess and judge who encouraged Barak to fight. (p. 79)	**Y.** Shadrach
26.	I prophesied that God would bring my people home again. (p. 156)	**Z.** Solomon

Possessing the Land

▶ Of all the people you studied in the Bible this year, who is your favorite?

_____

▶ Through this person's story, what did you learn about God?

_____

_____

_____

▶ In what ways has God helped you grow this past year?

_____

_____

_____

_____

_____

_____

_____

_____

_____

_____

Hymn Lyrics

And Can It Be

Verse 1   And can it be that I should gain
An interest in the Savior's blood?
Died He for me, who caused His pain?
For me, who Him to death pursued?

> Amazing love! how can it be,
> That Thou, my God, shouldst die for me?

Verse 2   'Tis mystery all! the Immortal dies!
Who can explore His strange design?
In vain the first-born seraph tries
To sound the depths of Love Divine!

> 'Tis mercy all; let earth adore,
> Let angel-minds inquire no more.

Verse 3   He left His Father's throne above,
So free, so infinite His grace
Emptied Himself of all but love,
And bled for Adam's helpless race.

> 'Tis mercy all, immense and free,
> For, O my God, it found out me!

Verse 4   Long my imprisoned spirit lay
Fast bound in sin and nature's night;
Thine eye diffused a quickening ray;
I woke; the dungeon flamed with light;

> My chains fell off, my heart was free,
> I rose, went forth, and followed Thee.

Verse 5   No condemnation now I dread;
Jesus, and all in Him, is mine!
Alive in Him, my living Head,
And clothed in righteousness divine,

> Bold I approach the eternal throne,
> And claim the crown through Christ my own.

By Charles Wesley (1873).

Amazing Grace

Verse 1 Amazing grace! how sweet the sound
That saved a wretch like me!
I once was lost, but now am found,
Was blind, but now I see.

Verse 2 'Twas grace that taught my heart to fear,
And grace my fears relieved;
How precious did that grace appear
The hour I first believed.

Verse 3 Through many dangers, toil, and snares,
I have already come;
'Tis grace hath brought me safe thus far,
And grace will lead me home.

Verse 4 The Lord has promised good to me,
His word my hope secures;
He will my shield and portion be
As long as life endures.

By John Newton (1779).

We Gather Together

Verse 1   We gather together to ask the Lord's blessing;
He chastens and hastens His will to make known.
The wicked oppressing now cease from distressing;
Sing praises to His Name—He forgets not His own.

Verse 2   Beside us to guide us, our God with us joining,
Ordaining, maintaining His kingdom divine;
So from the beginning the fight we were winning;
Thou, Lord, were at our side, all glory be Thine!

Verse 3   We all do extol Thee, Thou Leader in battle,
And pray that Thou still our Defender will be.
Let Thy congregation escape tribulation;
Thy name be ever praised! O Lord, make us free!

By Adrianus Valerius (1597). Translated by Theodore Baker.

Savior Like a Shepherd Lead Us

Verse 1 Savior, like a shepherd lead us;
Much we need Thy tender care.
In Thy pleasant pastures feed us;
For our use Thy folds prepare.

Blessed Jesus, Blessed Jesus,
Thou hast bought us, Thine we are.

Verse 2 We are Thine; do Thou befriend us;
Be the Guardian of our way.
Keep Thy flock, from sin defend us;
Seek us when we go astray.

Blessed Jesus, Blessed Jesus,
Hear, Oh hear us when we pray.

Verse 3 Thou hast promised to receive us;
Poor and sinful though we be.
Thou hast mercy to relieve us,
Grace to cleanse, and power to free.

Blessed Jesus, Blessed Jesus,
Early let us turn to Thee.

Verse 4 Early let us seek Thy favor,
Early let us learn Thy will;
Blessed Lord, and only Savior,
With Thy love our bosoms fill.

Blessed Jesus, Blessed Jesus,
Thou hast loved us, love us still.

By Dorothy Ann Thrupp (1836).

Holy, Holy, Holy

Verse 1   Holy, Holy, Holy! Lord God Almighty!
Early in the morning our song shall rise to Thee.
Holy, Holy, Holy! merciful and mighty!
God in Three Persons, blessed Trinity!

Verse 2   Holy, Holy, Holy! All the saints adore Thee,
Casting down their golden crowns around the glassy sea;
Cherubim and seraphim falling down before Thee,
Which wert, and art, and evermore shall be.

Verse 3   Holy, Holy, Holy! though the darkness hide Thee,
Though the eye of sinful man Thy glory may not see,
Only Thou art holy; there is none beside Thee
Perfect in power, in love, and purity.

Verse 4   Holy, Holy, Holy! Lord God Almighty!
All Thy works shall praise Thy Name, in earth, and sky, and sea.
Holy, Holy, Holy! merciful and mighty!
God in Three Persons, blessed Trinity.

By Reginald Heber (1800s).

When I Survey the Wondrous Cross

Verse 1   When I survey the wondrous Cross
On which the Prince of glory died,
My richest gain I count but loss,
And pour contempt on all my pride.

Verse 2   Forbid it, Lord, that I should boast,
Save in the Cross of Christ, my God;
All the vain things that charm me most,
I sacrifice them to His blood.

Verse 3   See, from His head, His hands, His feet
Sorrow and love flow mingled down!
Did e'er such love and sorrow meet?
Or thorns compose so rich a crown?

Verse 4   Were the whole realm of nature mine,
That were a tribute far too small;
Love so amazing, so divine,
Demands my soul, my life, my all.

By Isaac Watts (1707).

Be Still My Soul

Verse 1 Be still, my soul!—the Lord is on thy side;
Bear patiently the cross of grief and pain;
Leave to thy God to order and provide—
In every change He faithful will remain.

Be still, my soul!—thy best, thy Heavenly Friend
Through thorny ways leads to a joyful end.

Verse 2 Be still, my soul!—thy God doth undertake
To guide the future, as He has the past;
Thy hope, thy confidence, let nothing shake,
All now mysterious shall be bright at last.

Be still, my soul!—the waves and winds still know
His voice who ruled them while He dwelt below.

Verse 3 Be still, my soul!—when dearest friends depart,
And all is darkened in the vale of tears.
Then shalt thou better know His love, His heart,
Who comes to soothe thy sorrow and thy fears.

Be still, my soul!—thy Jesus can repay
From His own fulness all He takes away.

Verse 4 Be still, my soul!—the hour is hastening on
When we shall be forever with the Lord—
When disappointment, grief, and fear are gone,
Sorrow forgot, Love's purest joys restored.

Be still, my soul!—when change and tears are past,
All safe and blessed we shall meet at last.

By Catharina Amalia Dorothea von Schlegel (1752).
Translated by Jane Borthwick.

My Hope Is Built on Nothing Less

Verse 1   My hope is built on nothing less
Than Jesus' blood and righteousness;
I dare not trust the sweetest frame,
But wholly lean on Jesus' name.

Refrain   On Christ, the Solid Rock, I stand;
All other ground is sinking sand,
All other ground is sinking sand.

Verse 2   When darkness veils His lovely face
I rest on His unchanging grace;
In every high and stormy gale,
My anchor holds within the vail.

Verse 3   His oath, His covenant, His blood
Support me in the whelming flood;
When all around my soul gives way,
He then is all my hope and stay.

Verse 4   When He shall come with trumpet sound
O may I then in Him be found,
Dressed in His righteousness alone,
Faultless to stand before the throne.

By Edward Mote (1834).

A Mighty Fortress Is Our God

Verse 1

A mighty Fortress is our God,
A Bulwark never failing;
Our Helper He amid the flood
Of mortal ills prevailing.

For still our ancient foe
Doth seek to work us woe;
His craft and power are great,
And, armed with cruel hate,
On earth is not his equal.

Verse 2

Did we in our own strength confide,
Our striving would be losing;
Were not the right Man on our side,
The Man of God's own choosing.

Dost ask who that may be?
Christ Jesus, it is He;
Lord Sabaoth His Name,
From age to age the same,
And He must win the battle.

Verse 3

And though this world, with devils filled,
Should threaten to undo us;
We will not fear, for God hath willed
His truth to triumph through us.

The prince of darkness grim,
We tremble not for him;
His rage we can endure,
For lo! his doom is sure,
One little word shall fell him.

Verse 4

That word above all earthly powers,
No thanks to them, abideth;
The Spirit and the gifts are ours
Through Him who with us sideth.

Let goods and kindred go,
This mortal life also;
The body they may kill:
God's truth abideth still,
His kingdom is forever.

By Martin Luther (1500s). Translated by Frederick H. Hedge.

The First Noël

Verse 1 The first Noël the angel did say,
Was to certain poor shepherds in fields as they lay:
In fields where they lay keeping their sheep,
On a cold winter's night that was so deep.

Refrain Noël, Noël, Noël, Noël,
Born is the King of Israel.

Verse 2 They looked up and saw a star
Shining in the east, beyond them far,
And to the earth it gave great light,
And so it continued both day and night.

Verse 3 And by the light of that same star,
Three wise men came from country far;
To seek for a King was their intent,
And to follow the star wherever it went.

Verse 4 This star drew nigh to the northwest,
O'er Bethlehem it took its rest,
And there it did both stop and stay,
Right over the place where Jesus lay.

Verse 5 Then entered in those wise men three,
Fell rev'rently upon their knee,
And offered there, in His presence,
Their gold, and myrrh, and frankincense.

Verse 6 Then let us all with one accord,
Sing praises to our heavenly Lord,
That hath made heaven and earth of nought,
And with His blood mankind hath bought.

By unknown author (1200–1600s).
Adapted by William Sandys and Davies Gilbert.

Scripture Memory

Name: _____ **Teacher:** _____

Ls.	Scripture	Due Date	Signature
1	Psalm 111:1		
2	Psalm 111:2		
3	Psalm 111:3		
4	**Psalm 111:1–3**		
5	Psalm 111:4		
6	Psalm 111:5		
7	Psalm 111:6		
8	**Psalm 111:4–6**		
9	Exodus 20:1–3		
10	Exodus 20:4		
11	**Exodus 20:1–4**		
12	Exodus 20:7–8		
13	Exodus 20:12–13		
14	**Exodus 20:7–8, 12–13**		
15	Exodus 20:14–16		
16	Exodus 20:17		
17	**Exodus 20:14–17**		
18	Psalm 37:1–2		
19	Psalm 37:3–4		
20	**Psalm 37:1–4**		
21	Psalm 37:5–6		
22	Psalm 37:7		
23	**Psalm 37:5–7**		
24	James 3:13		
25	James 3:14–15		
26	**James 3:13–15**		
27	James 3:16		
28	James 3:17–18		
29	**James 3:16–18**		
30	Jeremiah 31:33		
31	Jeremiah 31:34		
32	**Jeremiah 31:33–34**		
33	Jeremiah 31:35		
34	Jeremiah 31:36		
35	**Jeremiah 31:35–36**		